Canada in the Classroom

Content and Strategies
for the Social Studies

William W. Joyce
Editor

National Council for the Social Studies
Bulletin No. 76

ISBN 0-87986-050-2

National Council for the Social Studies

Library of Congress Catalog Card Number 85-61551
ISBN 0-87986-050-2
Copyright © 1985 by the
NATIONAL COUNCIL FOR THE SOCIAL STUDIES
3501 Newark Street, NW, Washington, DC 20016

Table of Contents

Contributors

Janet Elaine Alleman is a professor at Michigan State University. She is co-author of *Teaching Social Studies in the Elementary/Middle School* and is an author of the new Follett/Allyn and Bacon Social Studies series. She serves on the College and University Faculty Assembly, on the Editorial Board of *Social Education's* Elementary Section and chairs the NCSS Rural Education Committee. She has taught graduate courses in 15 countries and frequently consults with public schools. Her current research focuses on the effects of global/international education on student conceptions of citizenship.

Richard Beach is Professor of Geography and Director of the Center for the Study of Canada at State University of New York, Plattsburgh. He was born in Montreal and raised in a French Canadian village in southern Quebec. A cultural geographer, Beach has taught various courses on the geography of Canada, including a course on the geography of Quebec, the only one of its kind offered in the U.S. His publications include a book, three atlases, curriculum guides and professional papers. He has lectured at 15 U.S. universities and is the only person in the SUNY system to have received both the Chancellor's Award for Excellence in Teaching (1976) and in Administration (1983).

Lynn Ezell was a high school student in East Lansing, Michigan, when she wrote her chapter for this bulletin. She graduated in June 1985, planning to enroll in James Madison College, Michigan State University, where she will major in social sciences with an international focus. A member of the National Honor Society, she also played volleyball for four years. Lynn lived for a month with a family in Vendee, France in 1984. With her own family, she has camped in most of the continental states and has made four camping trips to Canada.

Macel D. Ezell is Professor of American Thought and Language at Michigan State University. A historian whose major field is U.S. political history 1945-60, he has been primarily concerned with right-of-center groups. In a comparative framework, he has studied the Social Credit movements in western Canada as they relate to politics in the United States. He is active in the Committee on Canadian-American Studies at Michigan State and the Association for Canadian Studies in the United States. He serves on the board of directors of the Canadian Association for American Studies.

Victor Howard is Professor of English and Director of the Committee of Canadian-American Studies at Michigan State University. He is the author or editor of six books on Canadian history and literature. Among them are *A Canadian Vocabulary* (1981), a resource and curriculum guide for Michigan schools, and *We Were the Salt of the Earth* (1985), a narrative of Canada in the Great Depression. Howard is past president of the Association of Canadian Studies in the United States.

William W. Joyce is Professor of Education at Michigan State University. A former elementary teacher, he served as Elementary Education Editor of *Social Education*, chaired the Executive Committee of the NCSS College and University Faculty Assembly and served on the National Advisory Board to the NCSS Scope and Sequence project. Joyce has authored over 20 articles and 7 professional textbooks. His most recent publication is *Latin America and Canada* (Allyn and Bacon 1983), a middle school social studies textbook. Currently he is pursuing a longitudinal study of undergraduate students' conceptions of their national and global citizenship.

Victor Konrad is Associate Professor of Anthropology and Canadian Studies and Director of the Canadian-American Center at the University of Maine at Orono. He teaches courses in cultural and historical geography and in the geography of Canada. In 1976, he originated an interdisciplinary study of Canada now emulated in Canadian studies programs throughout the United States. His publications include more than 30 articles and reports and several volumes on Canada-U.S. culture transfer, historic preservation geography and native North American historical geography.

Martin Lubin is Associate Professor of Political Science at State University of New York, Plattsburgh, and one of the founding members of its Center for the Study of Canada. Born and raised in an ethnic neighborhood of Montreal, he regularly teaches courses in Canadian politics, Quebec politics, and Canada-U.S. relations at SUNY Plattsburgh. His most recent publication, "Nonfrancophones and the United States," appeared in *Problems and Opportunities in U.S.-Quebec Relations*, edited by Howard Daneau. He is currently editing a special issue of the journal *Policy Studies Review*, focusing on Canada and the U.S.

Michael Roessler teaches courses in geography and computer programming at the Portland Middle School in Portland, Michigan. Five of his computer programs have been published by Educational Activities, Inc. One of those programs—"Lincoln's Decisions"—won the 1983 Computer Software Award from *Learning* magazine. Roessler is currently pursuing a doctoral degree in curriculum and instruction at Michigan State University.

Wendy Sutton is Associate Professor and chair of the Faculty of Education at the University of British Columbia. A native British Columbian, she is a former elementary and secondary teacher and currently teaches undergraduate and graduate courses in language arts and literature for children and young adults. She occupies leadership roles in the Canadian Council of Teachers of English and the National Council of Teachers of English and also serves on the editorial board of the journal *Language Arts*. She is co-editor of the NCTE *International Newsletter*.

Foreword

The National Council for the Social Studies has long promoted adding a global perspective to the social studies. Over the past several years the Council has published bulletins on various aspects of world or global affairs. From the highly influential *Improving the Teaching of World Affairs* (1964) to the most recent bulletin on Japan, NCSS has attempted to identify and fill instructional needs in the area studies and international education field.

This publication on Canada is a reflection of NCSS's continuing commitment to our "neighbor to the North." Annual meeting sessions and *Social Education* articles have helped to inform teachers about various facets of Canadian society. This bulletin brings the story up to date, and the Council hopes that its distribution will promote greater interest on the part of all schools in studying and learning more about the enormous contribution that Canada has made and continues to make to the well being of our shared earth.

The bulletin has benefited greatly by the encouragement of all of the major Canadian Studies Centers in the United States. Special appreciation is extended to Brian Long of the Department of External Affairs, Government of Canada, without whose encouragement for Canadian Studies in the United States many of our impressions would still be wrapped in an Eskimo anorak.

A grant from Northern Telecom Corporation has made it possible to distribute this bulletin to all NCSS members.

Donald H. Bragaw, President
National Council for the Social Studies

Introduction

Adding a New Canadian Dimension to Social Studies

WILLIAM W. JOYCE
AND
MACEL EZELL

In the student-run newspaper of a large university in the United States, the heading of a photograph referred to "Ottawa, Quebec." That gaffe likely went unnoticed outside the local area, but when a U.S. president referred to Japan — rather than Canada — as "our best trading partner," one has to wonder to what extent otherwise knowledgeable Americans are unaware of Canada's significance to the United States.

Even in those states straddling the Canadian-U.S. border, misconceptions about Canada abound. Illustrative of this is a recent report issued by the Michigan Department of Education[1] on the results of a multiple-choice social studies test administered in 1984 to 4,100 students in grades 4, 7 and 11. One question asked 10th graders to list the nations through which they would pass en route from Mexico to Alaska. Sixty percent correctly identified the mainland U.S. and Canada, 14 percent listed the U.S. only, 10 percent listed Can-

ada only, and 13 percent identified the mainland U.S. and Guatemala. Significantly, the majority of students who took this test resided no more than an hour's drive from the Canadian border.

U.S. students can complete their public school and college educations without ever reading or hearing major references to Canada. The same students, though, are likely to read and memorize facts about ancient Mesopotamia and many other areas of the world, past and present. One need not oppose inclusion of existing subject matter in social studies classes to suggest that surely Canada deserves far more attention than it currently receives.

AN UNEASY FRIENDSHIP

These examples of our profound lack of knowledge about Canada are particularly disturbing when one considers that the U.S. and Canada are by far the world's best friends. Over the years these two nations have maintained compatible views on the broadest spectrum of international issues;

---

[1]"Test Shows Most Michigan Students Racially Tolerant," *Lansing State Journal* (September 23, 1984), Sec. B, p. 9.

1

A Canadian cartoonist's view of the United States-Canadian economic interdependence

they have enjoyed a long history of peaceful relations; they continue to cooperate in mutual defense efforts through NATO and NORAD; they have sustained the world's best trading partnership, comprising nearly $60 billion in foreign trade annually; they cherish and nurture close family and cultural ties; they share democratic values; and of course they are neighbors closely bound by geography and history. Indeed, the U.S. and Canada have so much in common and their destinies are so inextricably linked that both have an equally vital stake in a larger, more encompassing North American culture and civilization.

Have these strong, unifying forces encouraged us to take Canada for granted? Anthony R. de Souza, editor of the *Journal of Geography*, claims that (1) Washington's diplomatic effort is minimal, probably because our government regards Canada as a loyal ally that is totally within its sphere of influence; (2) the U.S. news media gives Canada minimal coverage — about two-tenths of one percent — except when an extraordinary event occurs; (3) U.S. educational institutions hardly acknowledge the existence of Canada (for example, few college geography departments offer courses on this nation and those courses tend to be superficial); and (4) the typical U.S. dweller regards Canada as our 51st state. Concludes de Souza, "Taking a country as sophisticated and as important to the U.S. as Canada for granted is a mistake."[2]

Though U.S. citizens and Canadians do have much in common, the two nations differ significantly in more than a few important respects. Compared to the U.S., Canada is a constitutional monarchy, slightly over 100 years old, is far larger in physical size but with one-tenth the population, recognizes two official languages,

gives more support to the fine arts and performing arts, and struggles to create a unifying national identity compatible with strong regional and provincial interests.

Canadians continue to be uneasy over the U.S. presence southward. They fear our extensive, often controlling interests in their business and commerce. Our nation's presence is keenly felt in the Canadian automobile industry, whose fortunes are closely linked with that of its dominant United States counterpart. During the recession of the early 1980s a Canadian ruefully noted, "When Michigan gets a cold, Ontario gets the flu." Canadians are vitally concerned over the failure of our government to enact and enforce tough new legislation intended to reduce sulphur and nitrogen oxides emissions, much of which are produced by industry in the Ohio Valley, swept into the atmosphere by prevailing winds and deposited as acid precipitation in eastern Canada. Not only are Canadians uneasy over their strategic location between the U.S. and the U.S.S.R. — they feel that their nation would serve as a buffer zone in the event of U.S.–Soviet nuclear war — their government is at odds with ours over the deployment of nuclear deterrents. They decry the debilitating effects of the flow to the U.S. of Canadian developmental capital, which they desperately need at home. They find it difficult to tolerate U.S. television, movies and publications, which they regard as a threat to an indigenous Canadian culture. Such influences, they argue, tend to overwhelm and dominate their own electronic and print media.

Several major sources of U.S.-Canadian tension were addressed by President Reagan and Prime Minister Mulroney at a summit conference held in Quebec City in March 1985. In keeping with the terms of accords reached at the meeting, the two nations will: (1) pursue consultation on acid rain pollution; (2) stop protectionism,

---

[2]Anthony R. de Souza, "Canada: A Neighbor Taken for Granted," *Journal of Geography*, 83 (September–October 1984): 194.

reduce trade barriers and facilitate cross-border trade; and (3) modernize the northern Distant Early Warning (DEW) line system. The two leaders also formally signed agreements that had been concluded earlier, including treaties that involved salmon fishing and cross-border legal cooperation.[3]

It is not surprising that U.S. citizens and Canadians view each other's nation very differently. Despite the absence of major differences between the two nations and despite the laudable history of mutual support and friendship, Canadians are worried about us — and for good cause! They are concerned that we know so little about their history, their institutions, their culture, their problems, their aspirations, and the complex web of relationships — political, social and economic — that bind the two nations together.

Two questions come forth out of this discussion:

1. On what basis does the United States build its perceptions of world affairs, on a belated, reactive response to crisis, or on a long-term basis calculated to prevent crisis?
2. What quality of friendship exists when one party knows the other very well but the second party hardly knows the first? Too often Canadians construe our ignorance of their nation as American arrogance.

LEARNING OPPORTUNITIES

But these negative issues are more than offset by the positive appeal of learning about Canada. It provides students with an opportunity to study in a comparative way variations of democratic institutions. The existence of a monarch and a parliament rather than a president and a congress is the major obvious difference. But there are other variations. For example, in Canada

voters do not need to exert efforts to register to vote. Before each election, an agency of the government enrolls eligible voters, block by block. In socio-economic policies there are also variations. For example, families with children receive a monthly stipend from the government. Housing, however, is not subsidized as it is in the United States, because Canadian taxpayers cannot deduct on their tax returns interest paid on home mortgages. In contrast to the United States, there is also a drastic difference in the amount of support that Canada commits to public transportation facilities. That is only one possible explanation of the relative healthiness of Canada's inner cities, which have not known the decay that some metropolitan centers have experienced in the United States. In education, Canada combines elements of both British and U.S. systems, yet it is more than a combination. It makes a university education for its young people possible for a considerably smaller personal financial investment than is required south of the border. And the Canadian government's per capita investment in the arts and in public broadcasting far exceeds that of the U.S. To encourage cultural groups to retain their unique identities, the Canadian government recently licensed the first Chinese-language pay-TV station. Called Chinavision, the station combines news, documentaries, variety and drama programs from China, Hong Kong, Taiwan and Chinese-Canadian productions.[4]

Canadian values regarding the role of the state in the affairs of citizens provide additional learning opportunities. Michael T. Kaufman, head of the *New York Times's* Ottawa bureau, observes, "Where the U.S. celebrates the individual, Canada celebrates order," and finds "the placidity and orderliness of Canadian life exotically appealing." The author claims that in his

---

[3]*Canada Weekly*, 13 (April 3, 1985): 1–2.

[4]*Canada Weekly*, 12 (October 24, 1984): 8.

travels through major Canadian cities he found no slums, no graffiti, no litter; further, the author reports these 1982 crime statistics: "the murder toll in Vancouver last year was 41; in Toronto, 44; in Montreal, 84 — compared with 668 in Chicago, 853 in Los Angeles, and 1,668 in New York."[5]

In Kaufman's opinion, the historical antecedents of the two nations offer insights into these distinctions. The U.S. Declaration of Independence postulates "life, liberty and the pursuit of happiness" as inalienable rights, while Canada's founding document, the British North America Act of 1867, speaks of the rights to "peace, order, and good government." Traditionally, U.S. citizens have been suspicious of governmental interference and championed the rights of the individual, while according to Mark MacGuigan, former Canadian Minister of Justice, in Canada the state was perceived as a "benign presence."[6] Accordingly, at the federal and provincial levels government has exerted a more pervasive influence in the lives of Canada's citizenry.

These are only a few of a great number of ways in which the study of Canada exposes students to different, yet not radically different, values, attitudes and institutions. To put it another way, learning about our neighbor to the north should not be understood as a humanitarian undertaking, but as a potentially fruitful investment on the part of American educators and their students.

THE SOCIAL STUDIES CURRICULUM

A major reason for our profound lack of knowledge about Canada is that our schools give that nation only minimal attention. A recent study by Joyce reported that major textbooks used in teaching U.S.

history, world history, and world geography devote between 1 and 3 percent of their content to Canada and Canadian-U.S. relations.[7]

Regrettably the recent preliminary Report of the NCSS Task Force on Scope and Sequence[8] fails to respond to the need to add more Canadian content to our social studies programs. The report specifically mentions Canada only once (in the 5th grade) in its list of recommended topics to be taught at the elementary and secondary levels. This circumstance will not improve unless the Task Force Report undergoes the rigorous study and debate that it deserves. It is hoped that this process will reveal that Canada and other nations in which our nation maintains vital interests indeed merit far more attention in our social studies classes than they are currently receiving.

Another recent publication presents a more sanguine view of Canadian content in U.S. social studies classes. Salinger and Wilson's report, *Canada in American Schools: A Janus Look*,[9] claims that there is growing teacher interest in Canada in some parts of our country. The authors cite as evidence of this phenomenon a new media awareness of Canada, the presence of Canadian investments and tourism (particularly in California and Florida), availability of instructional materials on Canada, and outreach activities of Canadian studies projects. Despite these positive signs, the authors note that teachers are not adequately prepared to teach about Canada

[5]Michael T. Kaufman, "Canada: An American Discovers its Difference," *New York Times Magazine* (May 15, 1983): 60–61, 80, 82–85, 87.

[6]Ibid., p. 80.

[7]William W. Joyce, "An Analysis of Canadian and Canadian–American Content in Major U.S. High School Social Studies Texts," paper presented at Annual Meeting of the Michigan Council for the Social Studies, Southfield, MI, February 25, 1983.

[8]NCSS Task Force, "In Search of a Scope and Sequence for Social Studies," Report of the National Council for the Social Sciences Task Force on Scope and Sequence, November 1, 1983, *Social Education*, 48 (April 1984): 249–262.

[9]Marion Salinger and Donald Wilson, "Canada in American Schools: A Janus Look," Report on a National Study on the Teaching of Canada in American Schools, Duke University Center for International Studies (Durham, NC, 1984).

6

from their own academic background or from inservice training. Indeed, they allege that familiarity with Canada may engender false beliefs about the nation.

ABOUT THIS PUBLICATION

The authors of this publication view Canada from a wide variety of perspectives. Contributors include a high school student, a middle school teacher, an authority on Canadian literature, a social studies teacher-educator, and specialists in Canadian history, geography and politics. We trust that the broad spectrum of views expressed in these articles will assist social studies teachers and curriculum developers in adding a significant Canadian dimension to the social studies curriculum in grades 5–12.

In "A United States High School Student Rediscovers Canada" Lynn Ezell reflects on her impressions of Canadian people and their institutions. Of particular interest to students and teachers are the author's insights into the variability of Canadian lifestyles, the high visibility of its diverse ethnic groups, vestigial remains of its British and French heritage, unique characteristics of francophone Canada, evidence of Canadian nationalism, and American influences on Canadian life. The author believes that our students' ignorance of Canada can be corrected once our schools make a concerted effort to add the study of this nation to the curriculum and stress the network of interdependencies, political, social, economic, and scientific, which unite our two nations. We hope that teachers will encourage their students to contrast their perceptions of Canada with those of the author.

The second article, "An Introduction to the History of Canada," by Victor Howard, traces major developments in the history of our northern neighbor. Though the author points out commonalities in the his-

tory of the U.S. and Canada, he asserts that there are certain unique dimensions of the Canadian experience meriting our attention. First, he states that prior to the establishment of the New England colonies in the early 1600s, English and French explorers and settlers had gained nearly a century of experience in cultivating the resources of what eventually became eastern Canada. Indeed, New France demonstrated a capacity for enterprise and achievement rivaling that of the settlements in what is now the United States. Second, Great Britain dominated over half of North America a generation prior to the American Revolution. Though it withdrew to Canada, Great Britain confirmed for posterity the enduring Anglo-Saxon heritage of language and institutions. Third, the author builds a strong case for characterizing Canadian history after the American Revolution as evolutionary and U.S. history of the same period as revolutionary. Finally, though both Canada and the U.S. experienced periods of immigration and westward expansion and conceived an essentially democratic ethic, the two nations lived these experiences differently and with different results. These distinctions are extremely important, according to Howard, for they document the unique and varied history of Canadians. Canada, which achieved nationhood well over a century ago, continues to assert its uniqueness and its identity in many ways. Teachers should encourage their students to carefully analyze Howard's assertions in light of interpretations of U.S. history that they encounter in their textbooks.

The third article, "A Geographical Perspective on Canada's Development," by Victor Konrad, disputes the notion that Canadian geography is an extension of U.S. geographical patterns. Indeed, the author asserts that most of Canada's vast extent of slightly less than four million square miles is a national territory unknown even to its own citizens, most of whom reside within 100 miles of the U.S. border. Using a series of carefully drawn examples, Konrad demonstrates how the Canada that U.S. visitors see has changed. Once based on a northern identity and articulated through images of caribou, Eskimo and Mountie on frozen tundra, Canada has become a complex of regional identities difficult to align or simplify coherently. The author regards this nation as a paradox of strong regionalism and strong nationalism, with urban settlements existing in wilderness, French farms beside English, traditional fishing activities coexisting with tidal power generators, and oil derricks near Eskimo villages. Konrad's descriptions of the ever-changing Canadian landscape dramatically underscore the importance of teaching students to view Canada not as an extension of the U.S. but as a unique nation confronted by unique challenges.

The fourth article, "Moving Canadian Studies into the Computer Age," by Michael Roessler, describes techniques for teaching students to design their own computer simulations on the acid rain controversy. Drawing upon his extensive experience in using microcomputers with his 8th grade social studies classes, the author proposes a generic model for student-designed simulations. He illustrates the function and use of his model by exploring the complex web of political and economic issues affecting Canadian efforts to persuade our government to reduce U.S.-produced airborne emissions that fall as acid deposition in Canada.

Roessler maintains that student-created simulations of significant issues affecting nations are among the most productive applications of microcomputer technology in the social studies classroom. Not only does this process help students to grasp the capabilities of computers, it also requires them to use high order cognitive skills and

provides meaningful exposure to contemporary issues involving science and technology, economics, law, pressure group politics, and international relations. The author believes that if his article stimulates the development of student-created computer simulations in social studies classes, it will have fulfilled its goal.

"Using Canadian Literature to Understand Canada," by Wendy K. Sutton, is the fifth article in this publication. Through sensitive, compelling examples, this author demonstrates how social studies teachers can use literature, particularly history and biography by and about Canadians, in guiding their students to a better understanding of those factors, geographical, historical, cultural, and social, that have shaped the character of Canadians as a people and as a nation.

Among the themes developed by Sutton is the process of immigration that has continued unabated since the days of the first explorers and settlers and the resulting cultural diversity characteristic of Canada's people. Dramatized in the literature are tensions between the desire to integrate into society and the desire to retain one's cultural integrity. This is poignantly shown in the author's discussion of literature on Chinese, Japanese, and Korean immigrants.

Sutton attempts to assist teachers in using Canadian literature in U.S. schools by suggesting grade levels at which tradebooks can be used effectively and by relating these resources to topics conventionally taught in our social studies classes at the middle and high school levels. These features of this article document the relevance of literature on Canada for extending students' knowledge about this nation while promoting their acquisition of vitally important language skills.

Beach and Lubin's article, "French Canada," explores the unique bilingual, francophone-anglophone character of

Canada in terms of its implications not only for the future of French Canadian culture but also for the entire nation. A major theme of this provocative article is that Quebec, historically the source of population replenishment throughout French Canada and today the guardian and protector of francophone culture, is the heartland, the *sine qua non* of French Canada. This factor, allege the authors, is a crucial component of Canada's struggle to sustain a cultural and national identity separate and distinct from that of their neighbor southward.

Teachers and their students will find that this article offers new insights into what the author regards as the inseparable, holistic nature of francophone language, culture, and religion. Describing this phenomenon in terms of the thoughts, feelings and actions of French Canadians who struggle to preserve their culture in the face of overwhelming odds, the authors maintain that the inexorable tide of assimilation induced by the dominant English speaking majority in Canada will in time threaten the existence of francophone Canada. Here is a vehicle *par excellence* for students to use in exploring comparable situations where cultural groups attempt to survive in the United States and elsewhere in the world.

Vital elements in this publication are the Student Activities sections immediately following the articles. Written by Janet Alleman, these sections provide teachers and their students with a variety of activities of demonstrated instructional value and are intended to facilitate the use of information from these articles in grades 5–12. Specifically, these sections seek to:

1. Enhance classroom applications of the articles and thereby bring the study of Canada closer to the student's life space.
2. Promote inquisitiveness in students and teachers about Canada and de-velop positive attitudes toward this nation's relations with the U.S.
3. Establish linkages between the social studies and other content areas—e.g. reading, language arts, science, mathematics, and the fine and performing arts—which add meaning to the study of Canada.
4. Facilitate competency in geographic, research, critical thinking and problem solving skills.
5. Involve students in computer simulations, role playing, debates and other learning experiences.

CONCLUSION

This is the first book-length publication on Canada produced by the National Council for the Social Studies. It was conceived for the express purpose of encouraging American educators to add a significant Canadian dimension to their teaching of social studies. Despite the growing Canadian presence in American society, as evidenced by increased media attention and burgeoning Canadian exports, investment and tourism, this heightened awareness may not produce this much-needed curriculum change. Teachers, curriculum builders, education agencies, and publishers may not perceive the need to add Canadian content to the social studies curriculum until they acknowledge that, since these two nations have more in common than any two nations on earth, it is essential that they become far more knowledgeable about each other. Our Canadian friends have taken the leadership in this quest. Even the most casual examination of social studies textbooks used in Canadian schools demonstrates that the United States receives considerable attention, if only because of the dominant role that our nation plays in Canadian political, cultural and economic life. Unfortunately, Canada does not occupy a comparable position in U.S. social studies textbooks.

Until the time when Canada becomes a specific area of study in state-mandated curricula, we invite the reader to carefully consider those grade level emphases of the social studies curriculum that can serve as legitimate points for adding Canadian content. Among these are the study of regions in grade 4; U.S. history and government in grades 5, 8 and 11, the Western Hemisphere in grade 6; and world cultures, global studies, world geography, and various social science courses at the high school level. Such topics provide opportunities for studying Canada in a comparative mode. Fortunately, Canadian Consulates and Canadian studies projects (see appendix), as well as exhibits at NCSS and other professional meetings, offer an incredible variety of free and inexpensive materials for use by teachers and curriculum builders. Indeed, few nations exert a greater effort to provide instructional resources to U.S. educators!

We hope that this publication will stimulate the reader's interest in teaching about Canada and suggest ways of bringing this nation into the social studies curriculum. In view of the traditionally strong bonds between these two nations and their common concerns, political, social, economic and environmental, the teaching of Canada and Canadian-U.S. relations becomes a vital investment in our future.

ACKNOWLEDGMENTS

Various organizations and individuals generously contributed to this publication. We are grateful to the NCSS Publications Board and Board of Directors for their steadfast commitment to the first publication of its type on Canada produced by this professional organization; to our talented authors for preparing high quality manuscripts despite stringent space limitations and deadlines; to the reviewers for their candid criticism and sound recommendations; and to the Michigan State University Committee of Canadian-American Studies for providing essential financial support. In addition, we owe our gratitude to Tom Turner, University of Tennessee, for his able service as our liaison with the NCSS Publications Board; to Charles Rivera, NCSS Director of Publications, and Anne Janney, Associate Editor, for competently supervising the production and dissemination of this publication; to Henrietta Barnes, Chair, Department of Teacher Education, Michigan State University, for her constant encouragement and logistical support; and to Hortensia Calvo and Kay Pratt for competently managing the myriad details associated with the preparation of the manuscript. For these valuable contributions, we are immensely grateful.

CHAPTER 1

A United States High School Student Rediscovers Canada

LYNN EZELL

Summer camping trips have been a family custom since I was four years old. We have traveled throughout the United States and into parts of Canada. Five years ago I remember driving north to Winnipeg and then west to Regina, Calgary, and Lake Louise on our way to the west coast. Two years later, going east this time, we went from Vancouver to Jasper to Regina before returning to the United States. Yet I do not have any outstanding remembrances of being in a different country, nothing that jumped out to tell me I had crossed a border. True, I was looking more seriously for the nearest swimming pool than for a difference in the culture or environment. I do remember seeing beautiful scenery everywhere we went and an abundance of open space. Besides, the people with whom we talked spoke English, the money was much the same as it is in the United States and the buildings looked like many of those at home. Certainly there was nothing to experience culture shock over.

WESTERN CANADA

Canada provided one special experience

that had to do with nature. In our years of camping, especially in the west, we had been warned about the potential dangers that bears pose for careless campers. Somehow the warnings made it particularly appealing to see a bear in the wilds; but for years, no luck!

When we arrived at the Jasper (Alberta) Federal Park, we met the same warnings that we had seen at Yellowstone and other places. We were bombarded with signs in English, French and international symbols: "Do Not Feed the Bears." In pamphlets handed out as they registered, campers were instructed not to leave food, scented products (such as chewing gum) or even locked ice chests outside overnight. No one could fail to get the message.

After we set up our campsite, my father jokingly appointed my sister "bear watch" for the rest of the afternoon. In a little while she was excitedly yelling, "There's a bear! There's a bear!" Sure enough, a couple of hundred yards away, one wandered slowly through the campground. It almost seemed that he was making a survey of potential targets for later.

In the evening we attended a campfire

10

program. The feature was a film about bears. One scene showed an automobile that had its door torn off by a bear because someone had left food open in the seat. When we returned to the campsite, we made sure that all food was locked carefully away and went to bed with bears on our minds. Sometime after midnight we were awakened by noises — automobile horns, beating on pans and yelling. The campers in the next campsite had not taken the warnings seriously and had left their ice chest on the picnic table. They were awakened by the noise of the ice chest being thrown against the ground to break the fastener. The people discovered the bear just outside their tent, eating eggs from the ice chest.

Another memory from the western trips concerned weather. Americans who watch television weather reports can easily assume that Canada is a very cold place. When we were planning our trips, we packed heavy clothing, even in the middle of summer. Sometimes we were in unusual weather conditions. At Lake Louise, we hiked up to snow fields and played in the snow in the middle of July. We also walked on the edge of the Columbian Ice Fields where we were told that the ice had lain frozen for centuries. Strangely, though, we were also in warm, sunny weather much like the summer weather of Michigan. We learned, too, that on the prairies east of the Rockies snow does not accumulate in great depths in the winter because the prairies are rather dry all year.

EASTERN CANADA

The summer I finished 9th grade my family spent a week in the Toronto area. At Niagara Falls we noticed bus loads of people who in speech, dress and general appearance were clearly identifiable as non-English ethnic groups. But it was also clear in hearing them talk that they were Canadians as well. In Toronto we walked through sections of the city where street names were posted in English and other languages such as Chinese. We ate at restaurants specializing in ethnic foods. I decided that immigrant groups were still more visible in Canada than in the United States. My father suggested that one reason for the visibility was that Canada, more than the United States, has tried to maintain the ethnic communities. This policy has served as a positive form of recognition of the diversity of the nation, not as a form of segregation.

I also noticed British influences, especially around the provincial government buildings and on the campus of the University of Toronto. Building names, architecture and portraits were only a few examples. As we toured the provincial legislative building, we saw the changing of the guards — men dressed in high, woolly hats who spoke in indecipherable military terms. Our guide frequently referred to British customs and history.

In the evenings around the campfire we discussed what we had seen: frequent subway trains that seem to run all over the city, extensive underground shopping malls, masses of people shopping downtown, the cleanliness of the downtown areas. I am sure the differences between the United States and Canada were more obvious at that point because I was a bit older and no longer concerned only with the location of a playground. As I realized that Canada was her own beautiful country — separate from her southern neighbor — I wanted to know more about her.

A JOURNAL ON CANADA

At home Canada was a frequent topic because my father was a member of the committee on Canadian-American studies at the university where he teaches. On several occasions we talked about how little Americans know about Canada and how infrequently Canada appears in studies at school. My father suggested that, since I had become interested, on the next trip I keep a journal to record the things I noticed, which led to this paper.

I do not believe I had ever before thought of Canada as a distinct country, because I never learned about Canada except in relation to the United States. The only Canadian history I knew was her role in the American Revolution. I had learned the fifty states and their capitals, but I never learned how many provinces were in Canada much less their names or locations. Wondering if this were ignorance on my part only I asked five friends if they knew the location of Canada's capital. Only one did. Talking to them in more detail, I found that names like Toronto, Quebec, Montreal and Ontario were all familiar to them but they did not know which were cities and which were provinces or where they were located. If students are taught in this limited way, it will be reflected in their later attitudes. I think it is vital that students have at least a basic understanding of other countries, especially one so close. In that way it will be possible to understand current political events that affect them — directly or indirectly. When students do not learn about something in school, they tend to think of it as unimportant. The absence of instruction in Canadian studies (history, geography, culture, etc.) unintentionally instills that attitude.

1983 ITINERARY

Our 1983 family trip to Canada began in Sarnia, Ontario, after we crossed the bridge from Port Huron, Michigan. We traveled northeast to Lake Ontario and drove along its north shore before heading further north to Ottawa. We then crossed the Ottawa River into the province of Quebec. We continued along the river to Montreal and on to Quebec City. We again crossed the river, which had now become the St. Lawrence, and drove towards the Gaspé Peninsula. Upon reaching Rimouski, Que-

bec, we went south to Matapédia and then crossed into New Brunswick. We followed along Chaleur Bay to Bathurst and then cut south to the Northumberland Strait, which we followed to Cape Tormentine, where we caught the ferry across to Prince Edward Island. We left the island by the Wood Island ferry, which took us to Nova Scotia. We drove west to the Bay of Fundy, then back through New Brunswick to Maine, U.S.A.

INITIAL OBSERVATIONS

To look at something in detail for the first time is a wonderful experience. The first part of the country encountered by all visitors is customs and immigration. It is easy to go right through customs without noticing a thing — awaiting the country on the other side of the booths. Since this is the first impression of the country, like meeting a person for the first time, it should not be ignored, because much can be learned from it. The fact that customs and immigration are present at all is a reminder that Canada is her own country. She has her own governing body, laws and traditions, which must be followed by visitors. It is much the same as visiting a friend's home. At the customs station one notices the use of metrics, the different architecture and bilingual signs.

LANGUAGES

Having two different official languages is a complication that does not occur in the United States and also one that Canada has dealt with in her own way. Both English and French are official languages in all the provinces except Quebec, where French is the official language. Spoken Canadian English still holds quite a bit of the English accent it started with. Other remnants are such words as *colour* (that end in *or* in the United States) and *centre* (that end in *er* in the United States). At times one sees words obviously influenced by American English —the word "hamburger" in French Canadian dialect, for example. It was not difficult to communicate with Canadians, yet it was easy for them to realize that we were not Canadian. To work around the bilingual barrier in Canada a very simple system has been developed. Generally, one hears English spoken first in predominantly English provinces and French first in Quebec. But so many people in both places speak both languages that one has a sense of being in a genuinely bilingual country. Almost without exception, places of business that cater to tourists are staffed by people able to speak either language. In several newspapers I noticed lists of job-opportunity advertisements for bilingual persons, especially salesclerks, tellers and waitresses. In some places, though, I did not find bilingual people: a movie theater in Montreal or grocery stores along the highways, for example.

On this trip, my father had a few moments of worry. We were sightseeing in downtown Montreal, driving our van because it was rainy that day. We stopped at a traffic light and a man came to the driver's window and started talking rapidly in French. Even though my dad can read French, he has difficulty understanding the spoken language. He was unsure of what to say — was the man telling him he was doing something illegal? He finally said (in English) that he could not understand. The man quickly switched to English and started asking questions about the camper because he was considering buying a similar one. What a relief!

American-based businesses with outlets in Quebec have worked out some interesting language compromises. Some rely on familiar emblems to communicate with a bilingual public and do not change their signs at all. Others show their adaptability with an American/Canadian sign like the familiar golden arches with a maple leaf on the inside. Others decide to go French all the way. The familiar face of Colonel Sanders is subtitled not by "Kentucky Fried Chicken" but "Poulet Frite au Kentucky." It loses a bit of its "down home" taste, but it gives the reader a good chuckle.

A visitor can also notice language differences in English. No matter where one hears English in Canada, it reflects a tinge of British accent. I was aware that I was obviously from "the States" as they say. One day while I was in a park, a man came up and asked if I had seen a Park Ranger around. I explained to him that I had seen one walking nearby a few times, but that he was not there right then. As I spoke, the man looked at me strangely and I could not figure out what was wrong. Finally I realized and said, "Strange accent, right?" He smiled and said, "Yeah — it's really weird." He laughed and he thanked me and went away. From then on I was prepared for such a reaction.

Another time I was talking to a young guy at a lake who immediately referred to my accent. He tried to "fix my pronunciation" and kindly explained my mistakes in English (mostly in the vowel sounds). I laughed and told him that was how people speak where I came from, and he sounded sort of funny to me, too. He seemed amazed, dropped the English lesson, and we began to compare differences in American life and Canadian life instead. To our mutual surprise we found that even with our different English, kids seemed to do pretty much the same things in the two countries.

EUROPEAN HERITAGE

Among other differences that visitors notice are the great number of references to the royal family of Great Britain. Even though Canada is quite proud of her independence and national symbols, the people also appreciate the British dimensions of their country. The currency carries pictures of Her Majesty. Roadways are frequently named after royal personages and the markers are coded with royal crowns. Prince Edward Island, obviously named for British royalty, is divided into three regions: King, Queen and Prince. It is possible to learn much about the Old World by reading place names and explanations of them. Many businesses take their names from British history or geographic locations. Yet Canadians' pride in their own country is also quite visible. American sightseers may be surprised at the number of maple leaf flags on places of business and lawns of homes as well as atop public buildings. Provincial flags are not only cheerful and colorful, but the detailed coats of arms symbolize both tradition and regional distinctiveness. Another indication of Canadian pride is the way the land is kept. In both cities and rural areas the environment is clean and well tended. Citizens take care to keep it that way and encourage visitors to do the same — through billboards, labels on disposable packages and numerous waste containers.

One of the cleanest cities is the national capital, Ottawa, our first major stop. It presents a striking contrast in architecture between modern North American and earlier European. The industrial or business sections of the city consist of shops and buildings similar to those in most cities of North America. New buildings utilizing many different geometric shapes, entire sides of glass windows and mirrors for modern appearance stand alongside older buildings in the conventional rectangular shape with regularly spaced windows. The public buildings, on the other hand, come from a whole other world. Their slender, pointed spires can be seen from blocks away, but their detailed ornamentation must be viewed close up. Most of the copper roofs have turned green over the years,

certainly adding an antique quality to their appearance. The interior of these buildings are more beautiful and more ornately decorated than the modern buildings. Stained glass, statues and intricate woodwork can be found throughout. Numerous portraits and murals tell much of the history of the country. The beauty of the buildings and the grounds that surround them make the capital a place where many Canadians as well as visitors come to discover the country's history. Symbolic guards are posted in front of many of the buildings and the daily changing of the guards attracts many people. For camera buffs, there are Royal Canadian Mounted Police — Mounties — in full red dress on horseback. Ottawa also has monuments and statues dedicated to those who have served Canada during wartime as well as peacetime. These are often surrounded by colorful gardens inviting visitors to come and enjoy them. Altogether, Ottawa is a place of history and entertainment, nostalgia and the modern world.

One strong memory of Ottawa did not have to do with buildings or politics — but food. The United States might be known for its fast foods, but I was happily surprised when I found a Canadian extravaganza. Walking down a major city street, we decided that ice cream was the next thing on our list. We saw a sign advertising an ice cream store in the basement of a nearby shopping plaza. We followed the sign and found an ice cream shop, but that was only the beginning. The entire basement was filled with fast food shops with a large common eating area in the center. Hamburger was only one of seemingly endless choices — chicken, fish, Chinese foods, breads, desserts. I felt like I was in heaven! My sister and I told our parents they could pick us up there at the end of the day. Teenagers also find such places especially welcome, not only for the foods, but also as social centers!

Quebec City. Old and new Quebec meet as 20th century tourists and residents gather in the Place Royale — the cradle of French civilization in North America — for cultural events. Here in 1609 Samuel de Champlain founded the first permanent French settlement in the New World. The spire of historic Notre-Dame-des-Victoires Church, built in 1688, contrasts sharply with TV antennas jutting from old stone houses.

All this is not to say that cities in the United States are entirely different. Some of our public buildings are also influenced by European background, but there are some subtle differences. For example, in the United States, one hardly ever sees lamp posts or crosswalks that are not rather standard. But in Canada, one notices a great variety. One also sees a greater number of outdoor cafes than in the United States.

QUEBEC

In Quebec, a visitor will see many re-minders of the province's Catholic religion. Cathedrals which tend to be very large and extremely ornate appear frequently. They generally have detailed stained glass windows, ornate carvings, statues, painted ceilings, massive organs and beautiful objects used in masses. Many of the churches are surrounded by gardens open for viewing and meditating. Almost all of the churches are open daily for tours as well as services. The Catholic influence can also be seen in other ways, the most common being names of streets, buildings, bridges, and rivers. People, too, often take saints' names. The other religious groups in the province are not highly visible. The French influence in religion and language is one of the strongest evidences of the French heritage.

Quebec City presents a miniature, purified reminder of the French heritage of Quebec — surrounded by a modern world with numerous other influences. On the surface at least, the part of the city labeled "Old Quebec" has remained virtually unchanged for centuries. The thick, fortified walls surrounding the old city, have literally kept the modern world out. The change between the old and new sections of Quebec is both immediate and drastic.

MARITIMES

As we drove eastward from Quebec City, we found miles of open country, numerous farmsteads, rural villages and — especially along the St. Lawrence — fishing villages. Much of New Brunswick and Nova Scotia lacked the affluent appearance of other parts of Canada. Local newspapers indicated that the Maritime provinces, like some parts of the United States, have long-standing economic problems. Uninviting housing, rough roads and decrepit business places are visible reminders. But the Maritimes also have their prosperous centers. On Prince Edward Island visitors see an Old World downtown area, prosperous-looking potato and dairy farms, brightly painted dwellings and quaint business establishments. On the island, tourists find churches that serve lobster dinners nightly in efficiently operated basement restaurants.

TIES WITH THE UNITED STATES

U.S. visitors will find familiar reminders of their home country. Many fast-food restaurants like MacDonalds and Colonel Sanders appear on both sides of the border, as well as department stores like Sears and K-Mart. At times one has a difficult time locating a Canadian movie. American-made films seem dominant. And television programs show many well-known American shows. In Montreal or Toronto, tourists can catch the Atlanta Braves or the Detroit Tigers as well as other National and American League baseball teams. The National Hockey League is also international, but because of different rules, football has remained separate. Conversely, curling, a game in which contestants manipulate 42-pound stones over ice, is far less popular in the U.S.

The presence of American businesses in Canada raises questions about the economic ties between the two countries. The number of trucks going in both directions indicates that the interchange is significant, yet American newspapers and television news programs have much to say about Japan, but seldom refer to Canada. A tourist will likely see some indication that the United States and Canada do have diplomatic problems. The Cruise missile (fake, of course) on the lawn of Parliament in Ottawa was a protest on the part of some Canadians against U.S. plans to test the weapon over Canadian territory. At customs houses and tourist information centers, visitors are given information about acid rain. Quite clearly, not all things are happily resolved between the two neighbors. For some reason, though, I had not heard about the differences with Canada before.

REMAINING QUESTIONS

During my stay in Canada I learned many new things, but I still have more to learn and questions that are still not answered. Many of them have to do with politics and government. I do not yet know how the Canadian Parliament was formed, how it works or how the Queen fits in as a part of it. Other questions have to do with the people. What do Canadians think about their government? Are they cynical or do they support it? How do they feel about having two official languages. Why do they have a metric system and the United States does not? And although I have picked up some tidbits of Canadian history, I still have no coherent overview of it.

CONCLUSION

Much can be learned about Canada without taking a trip there. The first thing for students to become aware of, I believe, is the country's geography. When you are familiar with the names and locations of the provinces and the major cities, it does not seem such a "foreign" country. New facts and ideas can be related to places and take on more significance. After the land is familiar, there are unlimited areas to study: perhaps a detailed look at a particular province or city, famous people, athletics in Canada, the major industries, Canada's response to world issues, the present system of government, the cultural influences contributing to Canadian life, and immigration patterns.

We have to our north a country to explore and understand. In the process we will learn important things about ourselves as well.

Student Activities

The intent of Lynn Ezell's article, is to provide the student with a look at Canada through the eyes of a peer who shares her first-hand impressions gleaned from extensive travel throughout the nation. Though students who are familiar with Canada may question some of the author's impressions, they are bound to agree that the article challenges them to gain new insights and understandings about our neighbor to the north.

Suggested strategies for students include the following:

1. Sharpen Your Map and Math Skills
On the outline map of Canada plot each of the places mentioned in Lynn's journal. Identify the point farthest north and compute the number of miles to your home. Then compute the number of miles from that northern point to the author's home in East Lansing, Michigan. Which of you lives the greater distance from the most northerly point? How many miles farther? At the rate of 25 miles per gallon, compute the amount of gasoline you would need to travel to the most northern point. Use local gasoline rates to determine the approximate cost of gasoline for a *round* trip to the northernmost point mentioned.

2. What Are Customs and Immigration?
The author mentions customs and immigration. What does she mean when she says, "The first part of the country encountered by all visitors is customs and immigration"? Investigate to determine the meaning of these terms. What are their purposes? Would you like to work in these areas? Why or why not? Find out if any of your friends have had any unique experiences connected with immigration and

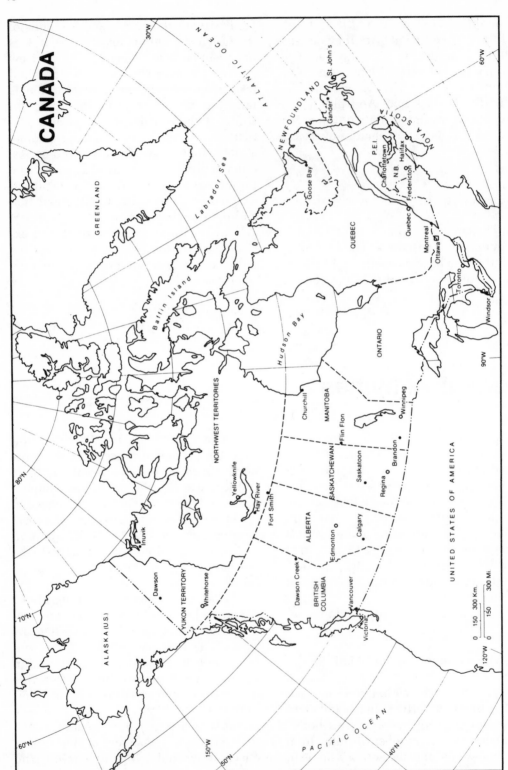

Courtesy of Center for Cartographic Research and Spatial Analysis, Michigan State University

Outline Map of Canada

customs in Canada or in another country. Encourage anyone with a story to share it.

3. How Are Our Neighbors Like Us and How Are They Different?

Reread the journal and then categorize the ways in which Canada and the U.S. are alike, and the ways they are different, and ways you are uncertain about, following the outline below. For every area you identify as uncertain, generate two questions you need to have answered before you can determine whether it is a likeness or difference.

LIKENESS	DIFFERENCES	UNCERTAIN
Restaurants specializing in ethnic foods	Government	Snow in summer Street names
		Question 1 Are there places in the U.S. with snow in summer? Question 2 Are there cities that have street names in more than one language?

4. What's Most Important to You?

The author mentions numerous places and features about Canada. Select one area of specific interest to you and investigate it thoroughly — for example, the history of two languages, Royal Canadian Mounted Police (Mounties), Canadian Parliament, why the metric system in Canada? The format for your report should include the following components:

Topic
Key/Idea
Review of literature focusing on the idea
Summary/Conclusions
Importance of the topic to a teenager

5. What Are the Chief Differences Between Canada and the United States and How Can They Be Resolved? (e.g., weapon testing, acid rain)

Lynn alludes to some conflicts that exist between the United States and Canada. Select one from the article or other literature. Describe the problem area thoroughly, indicating the positions of both Canada and the United States. Then develop a potential strategy for resolving the conflict. Finally, identify and describe the "pay-off" for each nation.

6. What Would You Include in Your Journal?

Reread Lynn's journal describing her trip to Canada. Think about the aspects that she elected to highlight. Beginning today, keep a journal for one week. Include aspects of your daily life that you are willing to share with a Canadian teenager. Decide whether you want to focus on likenesses, differences or both. At the end of one week share it with a Canadian if you have a chance. If not, share it with a teenager of another culture. Ask for reactions.

CHAPTER **2**

An Introduction to the History of Canada

VICTOR HOWARD

NEW FRANCE. BRITISH NORTH AMERICA. CANADA. By these three names, the five hundred year history of Canada can be addressed. From the first two, we understand that Canada has had two founding nations, France and Great Britain. From the third, we understand that Canada is a constitutional monarchy, related to the British Empire, but in nearly every respect a sovereign nation.

What follows is a sketch of the major factors and features in the history of this northern neighbor, a nation with whom we Americans share so much, but a nation so distinct from our own. Another country.

NEW FRANCE

Granted that Norse sailors found their way to the eastern shores of North America between 1000 A.D. and 1400 A.D., the real exploration of Canada did not begin until 1497, when John Cabot came ashore onto Newfoundland and Cape Breton Island. In the first quarter of the 16th century, these lands were visited by Spanish, Italian, Portugese, French and English mariners who fished, took Indian slaves, charted

coastlines and went home to Europe. Jacques Cartier ventured up the great river of St. Lawrence in 1535, as far as present day Montreal. By 1600 all competing interests had been successfully discouraged and France could extend its imperial design in the continent, calling the land New France.

The first permanent French settlement was launched in 1608 at Quebec City by Samuel de Champlain, explorer, cartographer and agent of the French crown. Champlain brought with him three great ambitions: (1) the discovery of a route to China and the East Indies; (2) the development of a fur trade, particularly the beaver pelts in demand by European hat makers; (3) the conversion of the Indians to Roman Catholicism.

Champlain and his followers soon realized that, by settling along the St. Lawrence Valley, they had at their disposal a remarkable water highway into the interior of the continent. While colonists to the south had to struggle across the forests and mountains until they reached the Ohio River, the French were situated along a lake and river system that led directly westward for thousands of miles. And the country was rich in furs. Although that trade was risky and involved regular struggles with the Indians, it was a profitable business and played a major role in sustaining the colony for nearly two centuries. Moreover, the search for fur took the French into the Great Lakes Basin and south along the Mississippi River.

Jesuit missionaries came not only to convert the Indians but also as guides, interpreters, explorers and diplomats. As early as the 1630s, when the Puritans were beginning to establish their "realm" in New England, the priest Jean de Brebeuf had already located a large mission among the Hurons.

However successful these initiatives were, the population of New France remained small. By 1670 little more than 8,000 French lived there. A century later, mainly through natural increase rather than immigration, that figure had risen to 70,000, most of whom were *habitants* or farmworkers employed on lands owned by an aristocratic class called *seigneurs*. It is from these 70,000 that the several million French Canadians living across Canada today are descended.

From 1690 to 1759 the French were involved in a series of wars with England and her American colonies as the two powers struggled for control of North America. The French believed that the British were moving illegally into the Ohio and Mississippi Valleys, where they had had no right since those regions had first been traveled by French adventurers. With Indian allies on both sides, these two nations attacked and counterattacked along, above and below the Great Lakes. The flaw in the French enterprise, however, was that nearly all of its supplies, reinforcements and communications came into the continent through the fortress city of Quebec. Capture Quebec and the French would collapse. And, indeed, this happened in 1759, when an expedition lay siege to the town and its citadel and, in a final assault, won the day, and — for a time — the continent.

The British Parliament in 1774 proclaimed the Quebec Act, which extended the boundaries of old Quebec west and south, recognized the seigneurial system, retained French civil law and the Roman Catholic church, and appointed a legislative council composed of French and English members directed by a governor. Thus, the French-Canadian presence was sanctioned and allowed to continue.

But by 1782 the British, having lost the American War of Independence, were forced to withdraw from their great empire to the south just as the French had a generation before. The Canada Act of 1791, promulgated by the British government, divided the region it now claimed into two provinces — Upper Canada, now Ontario, and Lower Canada, now Quebec. British North America, as it was called, profited from the arrival of some 40,000 "United Empire Loyalists," refugees who fled the young United States, bearing their loyalty to English rule and law to Canada. The UEL would, thereafter, be a prominent element in the population of Canada, in both reality and symbol a vivid reminder of the historical link with Great Britain.

BRITISH NORTH AMERICA

Life in Canada in the early 19th century was very much a frontier existence: great stretches of terrain sparsely populated; wretched roads and postal systems; few schools or churches; marginal incomes from farming, lumbering and fishing. Nonetheless, more settlers arrived from Germany, from Ireland, from Britain and from the United States, and accepted these hardships, whether they made their homes in Nova Scotia, New Brunswick or Upper Canada.

The French and the English, though living side by side, argued constantly and furiously over language, immigration policy, finances and governmental controls. The War of 1812 momentarily thrust these issues into the background as Canadians joined with British military forces in combat against the United States, whose president, James Madison, had declared war in a vague effort not only to prevent the British navy from compromising the freedom of the seas but to extend the concept of Manifest Destiny west and north. The conflict sprawled along such scattered fronts as Michigan, Niagara, Lake Erie, Lake Ontario, New York state and Washington, DC. It produced such legends as that of Laura Secord, a Canadian girl who overheard American officers planning an attack and who then walked for nearly 20 miles to deliver the information to her compatriots. After two years of weary jousting, the two nations accepted the Treaty of Ghent, which effectively restored captured territories to their original owners. The U.S. principle and dream of Manifest Destiny received a severe rebuke.

The second quarter of the 19th century in British North America was a busy era: roads, canals and railways began to unite the regions, if slowly; Montreal, Quebec City and York (later Toronto) grew into active commercial towns; secondary industries such as pulp, flour and ship construction flourished; several colleges and universities were launched. Most important, perhaps, the quest for "responsible" government gained momentum with English and French alike, particularly during and after the Rebellion of 1837, led by two patriots — William Lyon Mackenzie in Upper Canada and Louis Joseph Papineau in Lower Canada. British rule seemed so autocratic that several hundred dissenters went into the streets only to be quickly overwhelmed by government troops. But the incident sufficiently alarmed Parliament that it dispatched Lord Durham to restore order. In his report, however, Durham recommended the union of Upper and Lower Canada and the creation of responsible government, i.e., the Executive Council be made responsible to the Legislative Assembly and not to the Governor. While the Act of Union of 1841 created the United Province of Canada, popular rule was not forthcoming until 1848. That same year, Nova Scotia secured self-determination, with New Brunswick following in 1854, Newfoundland in 1855 and Prince Edward Island in 1862.

Canadians had continued to push west to the Pacific in search of fur, in search of water routes, in search of territory. Two mighty commercial ventures, the Hudson's Bay Company and the North West Company threw their outposts across the prairies, into the Rockies and beyond. Among the recruits to the North West Company were Alexander Mackenzie, the first European to cross the continent, and James Frobisher and Simon Fraser, who gave their names to the waterways they explored. And if the population and authority of the Canadian Pacific coast could scarcely be said to equal that of the Atlantic, it could and did respond when, in the mid-1840s, the Oregon Boundary Dispute occurred. The Oregon Territory between California and Alaska had been jointly occupied by United States citizens and the English, but when Yankee settlers rallied and called for its inclusion in the United States, James Polk, candidate for the presidency, sided with the Yankees and took as his slogan "54–40 or Fight." That is, the U.S. made it clear that the northern boundary of the Oregon Territory would be at latitude 54°40′ in contrast to the British preference for placing the boundary roughly along the 45th parallel. A compromise was reached in 1846 with the 49th parallel set as the permanent international line between the United

States and Canada. Eventually this would be called the world's longest undefended border.

Tensions continued to ease during the 1850s, once Canada and the United States agreed on a reciprocal trade relationship "for the mutual free admission of the principal natural resources of both countries." Although the agreement was canceled by the States in 1866, it was evident that trade between the two nations was inevitable and worthwhile and that special sanctions would always be forthcoming.

Canada's relationship to the United States during the American Civil War was curious. Canadians, by virtue of their points of contact and association with northern states, gave support to the Union even though Great Britain favored the Confederacy. One small band of rebel raiders moved from a Canadian hideout to attack St. Albans, Vermont, the only assault of its kind during the war. On the other hand, thousands of Canadians served with the Union army. And, as we know, the underground railway led many escaping slaves into Canada. The descendents of these slaves form one of the enduring keystones of the black population of Canada today.

Anticipating the cancellation of the reciprocity agreement at the end of the Civil War, still anxious about U.S. Manifest Destiny, concerned about the reluctance of Britain to ensure the military defense of its colony, and having determined the need for a greatly expanded railway system east and west, Canadian statesmen led by Georges Etienne Cartier and John A. MacDonald, "the fathers of Confederation," began to forge the means by which nationhood could be secured. The strategy of "Federation" was seized upon as the most appropriate for the numerous regions of Canada. A strong central government would still appreciate the need of these regions, soon called provinces, to have a considerable degree of autonomy.

And so on July 1, 1867, the British Parliament proclaimed the British North America Act, by which the Dominion of Canada — comprised of Ontario, Quebec, New Brunswick and Nova Scotia — came into existence. The several political bodies would thereafter elect representatives to the House of Commons while the other house, the Senate, would receive appointees. A Prime Minister would administer the country in consultation with a Cabinet, which was responsible to the House of Commons. The provinces were given such authority as marrying, taxing, borrowing money, maintaining prisons and schools, licensing shops, assigning property and overseeing civil rights. The federal government would look after such matters as legal tender, weights and measures, criminal law, the military, postal service, the public debt and foreign policy.

The first prime minister, John A. MacDonald, proposed a "National Policy," a grand plan that spoke of unity and progress and reassurance. Tariffs on imports would be raised. A transcontinental railroad would be built. A strong but liberal immigration policy would be set in motion. Extensive territories were brought into Canada's orbit: the Northwest Territories in 1868, and Manitoba and British Columbia as provinces in the early 1870s. Safety in these distant regions was assured by the creation in 1873 of the Northwest Mounted Police.

Unfortunately the peaceful momentum was quickly disrupted by a rebellion of the Métis people in Manitoba. Descended from French settlers who had married Indians, the Métis feared for their hunting grounds, their Roman Catholic faith and their traditional freedom. The Métis were led by a flamboyant patriot named Louis Riel who, in 1869, launched an insurrection that was resolved for a time only to break out again fifteen years later, after which Riel was executed for murder. Even

so, Louis Riel found a martyrdom un-
matched to this day in the west.

Prime Minister MacDonald's dream of a
transnational railroad came true in 1885.
His program of immigration, continued by
succeeding governments into the 20th century, brought hundreds of thousands of
new citizens from Europe, Great Britain,
Russia and the United States. The grand
design was to populate the western provinces, the prairies where millions of acres
of arable land waited for the plow. Called
homesteaders, new Canadians contributed
energy, imagination and dedication to the
west, and, because they were encouraged
to retain their original ethnic associations,
they furnished an exotic cultural mosaic
that persists to this day.

One important aspect of the "winning of
the West" in Canadian history is that it is
quite unlike the United States experience.
Whereas thousands upon thousands of
U.S. residents trekked to Oregon and California between 1840 and 1860, and thousands more followed after the Civil War as
the railroads came through, the overland
march in Canada occurred essentially near
the end of the century by railroad. Canadians have not given this experience the
legendary dimension that the United
States found in its western settlement. No
cowboys and Indians, no blue uniformed
cavalry coming to the rescue, no lean western heroes. Ironically, the Indians who
overwhelmed Custer at the Battle of the Big
Horn in 1876 found refuge in Southern
Saskatchewan! One of the few moments
when the Canadian West took on the aura
of a United States adventure was the gold
rush at Dawson City in the 1890s.

Not all the drama of the turn of the century took place in the west. Quebec faced
the transition from agrarian to industrial
life that confronted many other regions
and nations. The Québécois, by and large,
lived in villages where the families were
large and interrelated. The local priest

held considerable authority over secular as
well as spiritual matters. Self-reliant economically, the villagers pursued a serene,
isolated existence, their children seldom
finding it necessary to attend more than a
few years of school. Advanced and vocational education was almost unheard of.
Within a few short decades, this benevo-
lent, somewhat authoritarian society
would give way to new demands on its
people.

Canada came into the 20th century con-
fident, buoyant, a young nation with a
huge promise. The immigration program
worked, U.S. Manifest Destiny had been
permanently discouraged, the form of
government appeared stable. Confederation had acquitted itself. By now it was
also apparent that the country's political
leadership would be in the hands of two
national parties: the Liberals and the Conservatives, although the new century
would find these challenged by aggressive
young movements in the west and in
Quebec.

And then came World War I. Following
Great Britain's declaration of war against
Germany in the first week of August 1914,
Canada turned to the organization of an
expeditionary force, which departed two
months later. Over 600,000 Canadians
served in air, land and naval forces. Sixty
thousand fell. Safe from the actual battlegrounds, her natural resources of superb
quality and quantity, Canada turned to the
production of war materials and food,
gradually affirming her capacities as a
modern industrial nation.

A unique crisis for Canada during the
war years was the decision of the government, led by maritimer Robert Borden, to
replenish the ranks of the services by conscription. Though late in coming, this policy nonetheless irritated the divisions between the French and the English Canadians, because the former did not really
care to strengthen a commitment to the

A Timely Presentation

Jack Canuck: "Neighbour, what chiefly ails you is ignorance. Accept this little work, which, if duly studied, will save you in the future from making yourself quite so ridiculous."

The U.S. lack of knowledge about Canada has been a long-term problem, as witnessed by this 1884 political cartoon.

support of an empire that they did not appreciate or to the defense of another nation, France, for whom they had no real sympathy. This is not to say that many French Canadians did not volunteer, but many more resented and rejected the draft.

However devastating the losses in Europe, however contentious the conscription dispute at home, Canada did win a new stature in the British Empire and around the world. A Canadian Army Corps of several divisions led by Canadian officers won a distinct and honorable reputation. Prime Minister Borden was given a seat on the Imperial War Cabinet, just as each dominon was given membership in the postwar League of Nations.

The 1920s was a busy decade, at times as controversial as any in Canada's history. In the west, the new Canadians began to make their presence felt as economic, laboring and political forces. In 1919 a General Strike in Winnipeg, deemed inaccurately by the government as revolutionary, signaled a capacity for confrontation by workers that would never thereafter wane. Farmers pooled their resources and ambitions to purchase grain elevators and storage depots — in effect, in an attempt to bypass the intransigent railroad monopolies that had previously directed the farmers' access to markets. Out of this particular reform movement emerged massive service and consumer cooperatives — the Saskatchewan Wheat Pool is an abiding example — which characterize the prairies to this day.

In foreign affairs, under Prime Ministers Arthur Meighen and William Lyon Mackenzie King, Canada began to assert its particular brand of independence by creating a nine-member commission on the Far East, which was intended to monitor Japanese ambitions in the Pacific, and by withholding troops requested by Great Britain during a dispute between that nation and Turkey. The first treaty negotiated between Canada and another country was signed in 1923, with the United States, the subject being Pacific Coast fishing rights. By the end of the decade, the Department of External Affairs had been created at the federal level to develop and manage foreign policy.

Progress but also frustration marked Quebec's gradual accommodation to the industrial era. Natural resources such as lumber and water power had to be exploited, but the need to draw on foreign investors established a pattern of "intervention" that would continue for decades. The Québécois increasingly left their villages for life in the cities and towns, life that was usually marked by sweat shops, crude domiciles, disintegration of the family unit, dissipation of the religious life and authority. Much of Quebec industry and commerce came under the management of English Canadians who were better and more extensively educated for such careers. But the Québécois began to respond by renovating school curricula to include vocational and professional training. The whole experience made it more difficult for the French Canadian to retain his identity as a Québécois.

The 1930s in Canada are called the "Dirty Thirties" and if those years do not have quite the legendary status that they have in the United States, still the economic and social catastrophe is appreciated by Canadians. The worst circumstances were found on the prairies, where a prolonged drought further damaged a failing wheat market, and in the Maritimes, traditionally impoverished anyway, where declining export of fish and lumber proved devastating. Unemployment became a national tragedy.

Not unexpectedly, a growing chorus of demands was heard for political and economic reforms. By 1935, three new political parties had come into existence: the Cooperative Commonwealth Federation, essentially comprised of farmer-labor-socialist elements who found a national following immediately and who, under the revised name, New Democratic Party, continue to maintain a delegation of members of the federal House of Commons; the Social Credit Party, located originally in Alberta where its conservative philosophy took hold for decades; the Union Nationale, limited to Quebec and essentially conservative.

The General Election of 1935 returned William Lyon Mackenzie King, a Liberal, to office. It was Prime Minister King who took Canada into the Second World War. Once again, Canada mobilized. Once again, it sent air, land and naval forces abroad. Over a million served in the Canadian forces; over 40,000 died in action, including 10,000 airmen killed in the allied bomber offensive against Germany. Canada itself became a massive arsenal and granary for the allies. Among other contributions, it provided the sites for the Commonwealth Air Training Command, which prepared 150,000 airmen from around the Empire. The prime minister had his hands full with another conscription crisis although, as in World War I, only a relative handful of draftees were ever sent overseas. At the close of hostilities, for a brief time, Canada was the fourth largest military power in the world. A year later, her forces had been reduced to less than 100,000.

Canadians emerged from World War II a more sophisticated people, their industrial capacities enhanced by the war effort, their horizons extended by virtue of participation in a *world* conflict. The nation was now launched on a period of growth that would bring it to the point in 25 years of having one of the highest standards of living in the world. Along the way, it would earn the nickname the "Peaceable Kingdom."

MODERN CANADA

Many themes might characterize Canada after the close of World War II. Four are cited here:

- The "relaxing" of the Anglo-French monopoly.
- The emergence of Canada as an "honest broker" in world affairs.
- Quebec's tranquil revolution after 1960.
- The growing nationalism.

Whatever their feelings for one another, the English Canadians and the French Canadians view themselves as the "charter races" of Canada. In 1880, they provided 90 percent of the population; in 1930, 80 percent; in 1960, 74 percent. During the decade following the war, another million immigrants came to Canada, a quarter of them refugees from the catastrophe in Europe. Many preferred to reside in urban centers. For example, by 1960, 88 percent of all Italians, 63 percent of all Poles and 52 percent of all Russians, lived in cities or towns, as did, for that matter, 66 percent of the English Canadians and 60 percent of the French Canadians. A decade after the war, less than half of the residents of Toronto were English in origin.

This considerable shift in the ethnic composition raised questions about national unity and political power. The expression "mosaic" was given new meaning as was "cultural pluralism." The country appeared increasingly willing to urge ethnic groups to perpetuate themselves while taking their part in Canadian life and nationhood. John Diefenbaker, elected prime minister in the mid-1950s, was the first such officer who was neither English nor French.

Though relatively inexperienced in the articulation of its own foreign policy, Canada moved firmly in the postwar years to embrace the United Nations, to assist in the creation of the North Atlantic Treaty Organization and to join with the Southeast Asia Treaty Organization. Canada's diplomats soon won laurels for being exceptionally temperate in the increasingly tense Cold War era. They earned for their country the accolade "honest broker" for by instinct, discipline and intelligence, Canada was able to arbitrate international crises and to represent a neutral stance in the most difficult of circumstances. Following its participation in the Korean War, 1950–53, Canada has not waged war. But her soldiers and diplomats have observed wars and have patrolled the cease-fire zones of numerous battlegrounds. After the 1954 partition of North and South Vietnam, Canada provided delegates to an international team that monitored violations of the Geneva Agreement. Canadians have served as peacekeepers in Cyprus, Lebanon and the Congo, in Palestine, Egypt and Yemen. In 1956, because of his efforts at bringing about a solution to the Suez Crisis created by a joint British-French invasion of that region, Lester Pearson, minister of external affairs and later prime minister, received the Nobel Prize. And most recently, the Canadian ambassador to Iran, Ken Taylor, hid six U.S. refugees after the Iranian capture of the United States Embassy in Teheran.

The Quiet Revolution in Quebec began in 1960 following the death of Premier Maurice Duplessis whose long tenure as a "boss" had greatly restricted the emotional and economic growth of the province into the 20th century. Though the province was considerably urbanized and industrialized by this time, still its "managers" continued to be English, its resources exploited by foreign interests. The Liberal Party replaced Duplessis' National Union and launched a program of economic, political and cultural enlightenment that found energy in the populace's passion for being not French, not Canadian even, but Québécois! A quiet revolution but a real one.

Yet, there were those in the province who agitated for an immediate resolution to Quebec's status in Confederation, and independence at that. The Front de Liberation du Quebec, the FLQ, by 1963 had begun a campaign of terrorism that would kill Québécois and destroy thousands of dollars of property. Though many Québécois favored an independent status and gave tacit support to the FLQ, that organization never won more than a few dozen actual members. Its reign of terror came to a close in 1970–71 with the arrest of FLQ members who had kidnapped the British trade commissioner and the Quebec minister of labor, killing the latter. The federal government responded with the War Measures Act, which broke the FLQ and its supporters but angered many other Canadians because of its harsh implications for civil rights.

In 1967 the Canadians threw themselves a charming, buoyant birthday party. One Hundred Years of Confederation! Communities and individuals were urged to devise projects and activities by way of celebration. Two of the best known were the Science Centre in Toronto and the great Expo 67, perhaps the finest international exposition in North America in this century. Located in Montreal, Expo 67 drew dozens of foreign entries with lavish pavilions that attracted during the six-months of the fair over 50 million visitors who consumed 6 million hamburgers and 33 million ice cream cones and otherwise boosted the tourist revenue of the nation by over half a billion dollars.

The Centennial Year celebrated Canada and Canadians, but it did not exactly lay to rest the long-standing questions raised by many citizens: *What is a Canadian?* In asking this question, the citizenry launched a movement of sorts that came to be called the New Nationalism — a strong popular effort to comprehend the history and character of the country and to assert a pride in the past achievements and the potential of the country.

One might ask why Canadians, in the decade of the centennial anniversary, would conceive of a nationalistic spirit. Could the country not trace its history back over four hundred years? Had it not made enormous gains since 1867 in its pursuit of autonomy within the Commonwealth? Was it not a nation whose standard of living was one of the highest in the world?

Here are some reasons for that New Nationalism and that search for identity:

1. A long-standing confusion existed between the two Charter groups about their respective indebtedness to the mother countries, England and France. French Canadians felt little real connection with France since France had done little until this time for its "family" across the ocean. The English Canadians were still cognizant of the allegiance to the Crown and the Commonwealth, but the real contact with these institutions on a day-to-day basis was slight, although many Canadians were Anglo in heritage. The presence of a considerable number of citizens of neither French nor English extraction did little to ease the confusion.

2. The influence in Canada of the many interests of the United States had become overwhelming and overbearing, though how to break away was a challenge for which there seemed to be too few real solutions. The import-export traffic across the border was enormous; each country was the other's favorite customer. A growing chorus objected to the Americanization of Canadian culture through TV, movies, books and magazines, all of which were either exported to Canada or else beamed across the line. Paradoxically there was some real question about Canada's capacity to meet the interests and needs of its people in entertainment and "culture": the population was just too small; the United States was just too close by.

So much of Canada's economy had come under the direct or indirect control of U.S. industries and investors that a common complaint began to circulate: Canada was a "branch plant" of the U.S. Ironically, until Confederation, Canada had been a colony of Great Britain; now it was a "colony" of the U.S.

3. This resentment of "things American" did not begin in the 1960s by any means, but it may have reached its apotheosis during that era in great part because of tragic U.S. involvement in the Vietnam War. Many Canadians were sure that the United States was getting its just desserts in Southeast Asia.

The benefits of this New Nationalism:

- A new pride felt by Canadians for their country.
- A cultural explosion that saw the creation of new publishing companies, new theaters, new endeavors in the fine arts.
- A studied appraisal of U.S. investments and new legislation that more carefully monitored those investments.
- A broad and thorough new interest in the heritage of Canada, its history, its achievements.
- A new vanity: it was OK to be Canadian. And many Canadians who visited Europe and Britain then (and even today) wore a small Maple Leaf in their lapels so that they would not be mistaken for U.S. residents.

The 1960s closed with the Centennial celebration and with the emergence of Pierre Eliot Trudeau as a prime minister, who continued the Liberal Party dominance in federal politics. Since 1935 only once had a Conservative government been elected and then only for a six-year period in the late 1950s. Then the Liberals returned with Lester Pearson, a distinguished foreign affairs specialist. Again, with one brief interruption of several months in 1979, the Liberals, under Trudeau's leadership, held office until 1984. In short, that one party has "managed" Canada at the federal level for over forty of the last fifty years.

A charismatic person, a teacher and author prior to coming into government circles in 1967, Prime Minister Trudeau proved to be a controversial multi-dimensioned man seemingly well suited to the newly released ambitions of Canada in the 1970s. A French Canadian, perfectly bilingual, well educated and widely traveled, Trudeau made it clear from the outset that he was a "federalist," that he believed in Confederation. That he should stress this conviction did not really surprise his fellow Canadians, for one certain phenomenon of the coming decade would be the tensions between province and dominion, between Quebec and Ottawa, between the prairie provinces and Ottawa.

Across the early years of the 1970s, the Parti Québécois, led by a former journalist named René Lévesque, argued on behalf of a separation of Quebec from the rest of Canada — "Separatists" they would be called. And gradually the arguments began to convince a wider audience in the province. Among the reasons for separation:

1. The long history of subordination of the French Canadian in his/her own province by English Canadian "managers" and by foreign investment.
2. The danger of the loss of a pertinent, substantial French Canadian language and culture. Quebec was not France; it was Quebec. Quebec was not Canadian; Quebec was Québécois.

In short, Quebec became swept up in a nationalist movement of its own, derived from the quiet revolution of a decade before, in search — as Canada had been — for

its identity. Although the PQ, as it came to be called, was a provincial and not a federal party, Prime Minister Trudeau, being a federalist, could only look on with dismay. Already a language bill had been passed in the province that made French the official language there.

René Lévesque's Parti Québécois became the government of Quebec in the autumn of 1976, and immediately the new premier began to talk of a referendum in which he would ask the people of Quebec to decide whether the Quebec Government should negotiate some sort of separate status. An enormous public relations campaign was set in motion, in part to persuade Québécois that separation was feasible, in part to assuage the anxieties of foreign investors. If Quebec did, somehow, withdraw from Confederation, then would the whole country dissolve into a handful of angry regions? Would Quebec itself survive economically if it withdrew? Presumably, Canadians bound from the west to the Maritimes would still have to pass across Quebec. Would there be a border check? Would one have to have a passport? Who would pick up the garbage and the mail the day after separation?

By the time Premier Lévesque had prepared the referendum in 1980, the concept of "separation" had been adjusted to "sovereignty association." Some of its features:

- The only taxes and laws applying to Quebec would be those adopted by the National Assembly of Quebec.
- Every resident or native would have an automatic right to citizenship.
- Quebec would join the International Joint Commission (a Canadian-U.S. arbitration organization) and NATO, and would respect the agreement between Canada and the U.S. regarding the St. Lawrence Seaway.
- The Canadian dollar would remain the common currency in Quebec, but Que-

bec would establish its own investment codes and financial regulations.

• Free movement across common borders was ensured.

The referendum was held in May 1980 with Québécois going to the polls answer one question: "Do you agree to give the Government of Quebec the mandate to negotiate the proposed agreement between Quebec and Canada?" After years of debate, after years of waiting, the Parti Québécois lost the referendum. One possible reason: while the younger French Canadians approved of the negotiation, the older citizenry felt threatened by the changes implied and so threw their numbers against the proposition. Although the Parti Québécois retained its power after a general election the next year, the movement for a new status in Canada for Quebec seems, to have lost its momentum.

In recent years, both the western provinces and the Maritimes have expressed resentment over the so-called "Golden Triangle": Toronto, Ottawa and Montreal, where it is believed the real power and priorities in Canada are distributed. Both regions feel that they are often ignored by the financial and political leaders of the nation who live in those three cities.

The West is particularly disillusioned. According to Western Canadians, the Liberal Government led by Prime Minister Trudeau had unaccountably ignored them, scarcely going out of its way to flatter them or to court their support. The result has been a powerful sense of indignation that began to challenge the constitutional balance. And then there is oil, natural gas, uranium and water power. The West's natural resources in the last quarter of the 20th century are coming into their own, both as economic bonanzas and as political ammunition.

The energy crisis has affected Canada as it has so many nations of the world in recent years. But that crisis has been countered somewhat by the presence in Alberta of vast oil and natural gas reserves, by the discovery of uranium deposits in Saskatchewan and by the recognized potential for the exploitation of water power in Manitoba. The leader, for the time being, has been Alberta, which is sometimes called "Texas North" because of the presence of so many petroleum technicians who have come there from the American southwest. Given the development of its oil and natural gas fields over the past fifteen years and the rewards that have flowed to the province and the industry, for Canadians who seek new opportunities, Alberta is the place to be. The new wealth has meant greater influence in federal-provincial relations. A critical point of argument was over the Dominion's insistence that the price of Alberta oil per barrel remain below that of the OPEC charge. The Alberta "boom" seems to have halted, at least for the time being as petroleum surpluses build up around the world. Nonetheless the province remains a vigorous, controversial region.

The other three western provinces, though markedly different among themselves so far as history and immediate prospects are concerned, are still linked together by their anxiety over Ottawa.

British Columbia, long associated with such natural resources as fishing, lumber and minerals, has recently suffered so greatly from depleted markets and high costs that a bitter struggle between the work force and the provincial government has prompted other regions to examine that relationship more keenly. The Social Credit leaders in British Columbia have presided over dramatic reductions in the public service employees, of whom there are tens of thousands.

Saskatchewan, renowned for its wheat and socialism (the first socialist government in the Western Hemisphere was elected there in 1944), is the granary for Canada. Its populist sentiments, nourished by the many homesteaders who settled there from Britain and Europe earlier in this century, make it a unique political and social entity. And its search for oil and uranium deposits give it an industrial identity that will doubtless serve it well in the future.

Manitoba, though a veteran province, has long been frustrated by its failure to capitalize on its presence as a gateway to the west. This is partly the consequence of the building of the Panama Canal, which routed traffic to the Pacific with greater ease and speed. But the presence of the Canadian Shield, a massive rock bed that sprawls under most of the province, has made an agricultural economy something less than it might have been. Water power from the many lakes and rivers in the north is considered a great potential once it is harnessed. What is particularly distinctive about Manitoba, however, is the large ethnic population, all descended from the emigrations of the late 19th and early 20th centuries. In this respect, Winnipeg is the most "exotic" Canadian city in the west.

Despite recent efforts to organize a separatist movement in the Canadian west, there is little doubt that these four provinces are in Confederation to stay, though their collective enterprise and energy will surely transform Canadian politics in the next decade.

Dominion/Provincial relations were further strained during the late 1970s and early 1980s as the nation began to examine the prospect and significance of "repatriating" the Constitution. The British North America Act of 1867 had been conferred by the British Parliament, which thereafter retained authority over the Act, i.e., any amendments had to be approved by that body. Repatriation would return full authority over the Constitution to Canada itself. Given the nation's accumulation

of powers and rights that decreed its growing independence, repatriation was now in order. Its time had indeed come.

But a succession of meetings among federal and provincial leaders in those years revealed that such an achievement would not come easily. Although there was agreement regarding a Charter of Rights identifying fundamental freedoms and rights, not everyone involved shared the same opinion about the so-called amending formula. What combination of provinces could assure passage of any amendment? Given the history of regional autonomy, this question became crucial. As resolved, an amendment must have the support of seven provinces representing 50 percent of the population of all the provinces. After considerable discussion, bargaining and compromise, the provinces, with the exception of Quebec, reached an agreement that enabled them to complete the details of the new Constitution. On April 17, 1982, Queen Elizabeth II, who remains Queen of Canada, gave royal assent.

The new Constitution, particularly the Charter of Rights, will undergo regular appraisal and interpretations by both the citizenry and the courts. There is no doubt that it is perceived as a document that assures greater unity for Canada, and that it is in existence because of the strenuous efforts of Prime Minister Trudeau.

In early 1984 Trudeau announced that he would step aside as leader of the Liberal Party and as prime minister. A remarkable career came to a close. Governing with but one interruption of a few months (in 1979) since his election to office in 1968, Trudeau had been the longest-serving leader of a nation in the Western Bloc. Though not always popular, he is nonetheless one of the great statesmen Canada has produced in this century.

The process by which Trudeau was replaced in office, a process unlike any in the

United States, reflects the uniqueness of Canada. First, Trudeau turned over leadership of the Liberal Party to a successor who had been elected by the party at a convention. Then, since the Liberals held a majority of seats in the House of Commons, that person became prime minister. The new prime minister shortly thereafter called a general election and the people of Canada had the opportunity to choose a leader from the candidates provided by the national parties in Parliament — the Liberals, the Progressive Conservatives and the New Democrats. What is implicit in this arrangement is that the prime minister of Canada must first be elected to the House of Commons, then elected leader of his party and then, if his party is in the majority, be elected leader of the nation.

In actuality, Trudeau was succeeded by John Turner, a former cabinet minister who, as leader of the Liberals, then became prime minister. In September 1984, as the result of a general election, the Tory Party lead by Brian Mulroney, became the government in power. Turner continued as leader of the Liberals and thus leader of the opposition in the House of Commons.

CONCLUSION

Certain dimensions in Canadian history should be quickly reviewed, primarily because U.S. residents seldom realize that:
1. By the time the New England colonies were coming into being in the early 17th century, English and French explorers and settlers had already gained nearly a century's experience in cultivating the resources of what would one day become eastern Canada. In time, New France would demonstrate a capacity for enterprise and achievement that was no less brilliant than the settlements to the south.
2. For a generation Great Britain held effective authority over half of North America, following their conquest in 1759 and prior to the American Revolution. Though it withdrew to Canada, Great Britain confirmed for posterity the enduring Anglo-Saxon heritage of the American "race": its language, its institutions.
3. Canada's history after the American Revolution may be interpreted according to the laws of *evolution;* the United States' history according to the energies set loose by *revolution.*
4. While Canada and the United States share the experiences of accommodating great numbers of immigrants, of a westward expansion and of conceiving an essentially democratic ethic, the two nations have lived these experiences in different ways with different results.

The history of Canada has been, in a real sense, the history of its attempts to confirm nationhood and to assert its particular place in the British Empire and on this continent. Nationhood came over a century ago, but Canada continues and will continue in its assertion of its uniqueness, its identity.

Student Activities

Howard's article provides the reader with a historical overview of Canada's development. The author illustrates how the 500 years of Canada's history can be meaningfully addressed by three names: New France, British North America and Canada. Suggested strategies for further examining the multiple facets of Canada's history include the following:

1. Is This Debatable?

Preparing for a debate is an excellent way to clarify issues. After researching the origins and conduct of the War of 1812, prepare for a brief debate between a U.S. participant and a Canadian participant. What are some of the issues worth arguing? (Think about the style for each debater). Key points to keep in mind in preparing and presenting a debate include:

- Debates are sometimes used as a means of facing a controversial issue directly.
- A debate focuses attention on extreme viewpoints regarding an issue.
- Acquaintance with the extreme viewpoints may help you realize the extent of differing opinions on a subject. Debates may properly be used to expose or clarify those extremes.
- Debates require of participants, and encourage among listeners, an either-or outlook toward an issue.
- No more than three students should be selected to serve on each debating team.
- Adequate class time should be allotted for exploration of the issue and time allotments for each speaker should be enforced.
- Speakers should not be interrupted, but open discussion can follow immediately after the debate.
- Probably not more than one class period should be allotted for a debate.

- A debate issue should be stated clearly, specifically and pointedly.
- Each debater should thoughtfully — with adequate documentation — prepare his/her side of the issue. Debating tactics should remain secondary to clear and forthright presentations of points of view and substantiating of facts.

2. How Did It Feel to Be an Immigrant to Canada in the Early 20th Century?

Investigate the Canadian immigration policies at the turn of the century. Then identify the groups of individuals and approximate numbers (determine by percents) that settled in Canada. When you have acquired the background data, develop role cards for you and your peers. An example:

VISA

Age: 28
Occupation: Farmer
Health: Good
Sex: Male
Religion: Lutheran
Nationality: German

Set up the classroom to resemble an early immigration "office," where no talking is allowed. Two of you can volunteer to be immigration officers. The other students should each draw a data card from the back and proceed directly to the front of the room. Immigrants will proceed through the line while the officers decide whether they will be allowed to enter the country.

After the simulation has concluded, the teacher can lead a discussion. Suggested questions are:

- How did you feel standing in line waiting your turn?

- What problems did you encounter as you sought entry?
- Was everyone admitted? Why? Why not? If not, describe the pattern.
- How did you feel about launching a life in another country?

Most immigrants came to stay in the new world. Standish O'Grady, however, arrived in 1836, looked around, saw what follows and went back to Ireland. Read the poem he wrote and be prepared to discuss it.

From the Immigrant[1]

Bleak, barren spot, ah! Why should I
    forsake
A fertile land to threat thy worthless
    brate?
Labor alore they fertile land surveys,
Breathes the dull round, or prematurely
    pays
A hard won pittance, through distress and
    toil,
Still doomed again to lavish on thy soil;
O land! that's slothful, miserable spot,
Ungracious sandbank! May it be my lot
Remote to dwell 'mong happier kind
    abodes,
And leave to grasshoppers a land of toads!
    Thou barren waste; unprofitable strand,
Where hemlocks broad in unproductive
    land,
Whose frozen air on one bleak winter's
    night
Can metamorphose dark brown hares to
    white!
Whose roads are rivers, o'er your
    fountains
See icebergs form your shining mountains
And drifted snow, from arctic regions,
Gives sheer employment to Canadians,
Here roads ne'er known for many a
    summer,
And now past o'er by each new comer,
All wrought one night, nor made of stone
    or gravel,
Complete withal and next day fit to travel,
Here forests crowd, unprofitable lumber,
O'er fruitless lands indefinite as number;

[1]Originally published in 1842, this poem has been reprinted in Victor Howard's *A Canadian Vocabulary* (East Lansing, MI: Michigan State University, 1981), 41-42.

Where birds scarce light, and with the
    north winds veer
On wings of wind, and quickly disappear,
Here the rough Bear subsists his winter
    year.

- Why do you think Standish returned to Ireland?
- During what time of the year did he leave? What evidence does the poem provide?
- What were three impressions Standish had of Canada? Do you think they were valid or invalid? Be prepared to explain your answers.

3. Creating a Cartoon

Select five political cartoons from a recent newspaper. What techniques did the cartoonists use? Then look at the cartoons in this Bulletin. Think about the special interest groups of Canada and how they were split on the issue of Confederation. Design a cartoon to illustrate this.

Key points to remember in designing a cartoon include:

- Most cartoons of social significance deal with political themes, though some are related to economic or other social matters.
- The value of cartoons used in social studies classes lies in the ideas represented rather than the symbols.
- A cartoon represents a particular viewpoint or interpretation and contains persuasive or propagandistic material.

Share your cartoon with a peer. Then display all of the cartoons on the bulletin board. How are they alike? How are they different?

4. Create a Time Line

Make a list of ten significant events in Canadian history that you feel are worth remembering. Then construct a time line that includes the dates and words, pictures, or both that accurately communicate the historical development of this nation to the north. The challenge is to design a time line that will be eye-catching and guarantee that the reader will *remember* the significant events.

5. What Is the Correlation Between Resources and History?

See Student Activities Chapter 1 for an outline map of Canada. Secure a copy of this map and make a natural resource map of Canada. After you have completed that task, pinpoint on the map six historical events that seem to correspond to resources available. Below the map, briefly describe how each resource impacted on the historical development of Canada. If time permits, briefly describe the status of each natural resource today. Does it have political implications? Does Canada's economy depend on it? Is there a sufficient supply? It is renewable or non-renewable? Include any unique characteristics of the resource that you are able to discover.

6. Who Won The War of 1812?

Obtain library books that describe the history of North America. Compare and contrast the accounts of the War of 1812 and the events that followed. Which nation do you think won the war? Write a one-page essay as a response to the question. Document your answer.

7. Where is the "Center" of the World?

Often textbook and reference materials are biased due to the author's orientation or perspective. Locate Canadian and U.S. sources to determine if and where there are discrepancies. For example, are there instructional materials that show Canada at the center of world maps? Is the United States in a central position in either U.S. or Canadian instructional materials?

In two or more paragraphs, explain your views on this matter. For example, is this a serious issue? Why or why not? How should it be handled in the classroom? Cite examples (where appropriate) to show congruence of concepts and discrepancies.

CHAPTER **3**

A Geographical Perspective on Canada's Development

VICTOR KONRAD

When Canada is considered by neighbors in the United States, Canadian geography usually is regarded as an extension of U.S. geographical patterns. Major regions of the United States, the parallel ridges of Western Cordillera, the Great Plains and the Appalachians extend into Canada. Most Canadians live just the other side of the Great Lakes and St. Lawrence River, in towns and cities with familiar businesses and similar houses. Consistent rural landscapes are found in between. Indeed, a casual glance across the border confirms that Canadians developed their land in harmony with the United States.

Yet a look beyond the borderlands of shared experience and adjusted livelihood reveals a distinct geography characterized by landforms unknown, climates not experienced and settlement adaptations never required in the continental United States. Most of Canada's vast extent of more than 3,851,000 square miles is a national territory unknown even to its own citizens who live mainly within 100 miles of the United States border. Few Canadians have ventured to the Arctic archipelago of remnant continental glaciation, seen the tundra that

annually breeds the western hemisphere's migratory flocks, experienced summer's constant daylight north of 60°, or stayed to winter the grim Canadian Shield. Yet all are touched by a geography differentiated from that of the United States by its northern characteristics, insularity and dependency. These prevailing themes of Canada's geography describe a land where winter never fully disappears and explain a regional evolution of isolated settlement and a national system of far-stretching life-lines.

In Canada there is no escape from the northern character of the country's geography, for all of Canada is either in the north or "of the North."[1] Because of its northern position, Canada spends more time frozen than thawed. This condition is prolonged by the high albedo, or proportion of radiation reflected by white winter's snow and ice, and the continental arctic air mass that prevails in the saucer of the Canadian land mass centered on Hudson Bay. In spite of maritime air masses

---

[1]W.C. Wonders, ed. *Canada's Changing North* (Toronto: McClelland and Stewart, 1971), 351.

that reach Canada from the Pacific and less frequently from the Gulf of Mexico to moderate temperatures and bring precipitation, most of the country is characterized by continental extremes of long cold and dry winters alternating with short and warm summers. Moderating effects along Pacific and Atlantic coasts are confined by mountain ranges. Only in the Great Lakes region does open water continue into the winter to provide a moderating effect on the interior land. In the far north, ground as well as water freezes to great depths. Permafrost or permanently frozen ground may extend to depths in excess of 1,000 feet on northernmost Ellsmere Island and characterizes nearly 50 percent of Canada's land area. In the far north, permafrost is continuous, whereas in the subarctic it becomes discontinuous forming a patchwork of elevated frozen areas separated by ice-free lowlands. During the brief Arctic summer, the upper or active layer thaws and may produce, in poorly drained areas, impassable masses of organic terrain known as muskeg. Muskeg, snow, floating ice and the myriad of small lakes clustered in the Canadian Shield store the major portion of the continent's water but release it grudgingly. Water and potential mineral and organic resources of the North remain preserved yet out of reach because of the pervasive winter, which perhaps more than any other characteristic reflects the Canadian condition.[2]

The Canadian condition is also insularity. As if projected from the polar archipelago, the islands of Canadian settlement remain isolated along 7,200 kilometers (4,500 miles) of endless boundary with the United States.[3] Separated on occasion by water and ice but more often by rock, muskeg and forest, small coastal refuges or

expansive regions of agricultural settlement all suffer the tyranny and cost of distance from each other. Newfoundland's isolated coastal villages reflect the national condition at a regional level. There and in the Maritime provinces of Nova Scotia, Prince Edward Island and New Brunswick, communities along rockbound coasts maintained uncertain sea connections with each other and the outside until recent road and air routes were established at considerable cost. Paradoxically, these routes served to move residents to larger islands in the region — to Halifax, St. John's and Moncton where opportunity is concentrated — and to leave the smaller islands to fade from the archipelago. Lowland Quebec and Ontario predominate in the island chain. More closely linked to the industrial northeastern United States than either the Canadian east or west, English Ontario and French Quebec remain isolated by language, tradition and aspiration. A different distance of granite shield and interminable black spruce insures tenuous links with Canada's most expansive block of agricultural settlement. As in the Great Plains south of the border, the sectional survey extends linked farms from the forest fringing the Shield in eastern Manitoba to the Rocky Mountain wall in western Alberta. The Rockies and successive parallel ridges extend to the ocean, isolating valley communities from each other and maintaining a distinct center of blended California culture and British remnants on Canada's Pacific slope.

Island chains are characteristically dependencies, and the islands of the Canadian archipelago appear to conform. Within the Confederation, small Prince Edward Island, employment-poor Newfoundland

---

[2]A brief yet comprehensive discussion of Canada's northern character and conditions sets the theme for a major text on Canadian geography: Louis-Edmond Hamelin, *Canada, A Geographical Perspective* (Toronto: Wiley, 1973), 3–38.

[3]The metaphor of archipelago aptly summarizes the isolation and regional distinction of Canadian settlement. See R. Cole Harris, "Regionalism and the Canadian Archipelago," in L. D. McCann, ed., *A Geography of Canada, Heartland and Hinterland* (Scarborough: Prentice-Hall, 1982), 459–484.

and land resource-oriented Saskatchewan all need the capital, manufactured goods and government insurance provided by the population and production center. This relationship of heartland to hinterland, of center to periphery, describes the contrasting landscapes of metropolis and resource territory and explains the process of urban concentration and increasing dependency of the resource regions that characterize Canada.[4] As the industrial *heartland* of lowland Ontario and Quebec expands, it concentrates capital and manufacturing, attracts population, extends internal as well as external markets, and generally leads the nation in economic growth. Although *hinterland* cities process some resources, their role is to transport resources to the heartland cities for manufacturing and to distribute manufactured goods received from the heartland. Consequently, hinterland cities grow more slowly than urban places in the heartland, which support higher growth-inducing activities, such as manufacturing and finance, as well as sustaining wholesale, retail and transportation functions. The result is increasing concentration of wealth and power in the heartland and metropolitan dominance of Toronto and Montreal in Canada. But these major cities and all of the components of heartland and hinterland are dependencies in another sense. Whether through connections in Toronto banks or through direct transfers of goods between Bangor, Maine, and Fredericton, New Brunswick, Canadians and Canadian regional entities are all tied to the United States. Since Confederation, Canada has traded its colonial origins for an economy integrated with that of its neighbor and controlled by U.S.-based multinational corporations. In spite of Canadian attempts to establish a separate

identity, the country remains strongly influenced by U.S. mass culture as well as economic control. Yet such a high degree of dependency has not restrained Canada from attaining an international reputation in world affairs, developing its own aggressive and multinational corporations, and providing its citizens with one of the highest standards of living in the world. Viewed as dependency, archipelago or northern expanse, Canada remains an enigma worthy of exploration and geographical study.

A COUNTRY OF DISTINCT REGIONS

Canada's physical environment continues to provide the basis for differentiating major regions of the country. Boundaries of natural landscape zones remain distinct after centuries of human attempts to ameliorate differences among them. Although not all as dramatic as the sudden thrust of Cordilleran ranges above the Great Plains, the crystalline edge of Canadian Shield granite, the "tree line" between tundra and forest and the boundary of permanent ice also mark environmental borders beyond human control.[5]

Landforms establish the template for designating Canada's regions. These topographic or physiographic divisions (figure 1) are general categories of geological structures that persist as landforms at the earth's surface. Dominant is the *Canadian Shield* of very old and resistant Precambrian granites and gneisses which extends throughout eastern and central Canada. A rolling landscape of glacially rounded mountains and innumerable lakes, it collars the *Hudson Bay Lowland* of sedimentary rocks horizontally overlaying the Shield. The Hudson Bay Lowland sediments occupy the center of the saucer-

---

[4]This theme forms the major organizing principle for the most recent geography text on Canada: L. D. McCann, *Heartland and Hinterland*. See specifically pp. 3–35.

[5]For a readable and well-illustrated introduction to Canada's natural landscapes see J. Brian Bird, *The Natural Landscapes of Canada*, 2nd ed. (Toronto: Wiley, 1980).

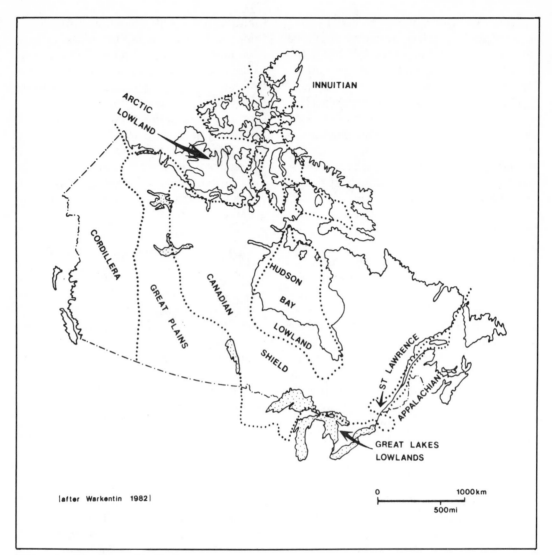

Figure 1.   Physiographic Regions

shaped Shield, whereas elevated edges of
the Shield meet other sedimentary regions
of the *Great Plains* in the west, *Arctic Lowlands* in the north and *Great Lakes–St.
Lawrence Lowlands* in the south. Border-
ing these restricted lowlands and bound-
ing Canada are the *Innuitian* mountains in
the north, the parallel ranges of the *Cordillera* to the west and the older, worn *Appalachian* ridges to the east.

Extremely cold climates sustain permanent ice in the Innuitian mountains and
northern Cordillera ranges (figure 2). Peri-
glacial or near glacial conditions prevail
throughout much of Arctic Canada and in
the high altitudes of the Cordillera, but
latitude or distance to the equator then
prevails to establish bands of subarctic and
humid continental climates across Canada. The interplay of warm, moisture-
laden air with cold ocean currents keeps
the west coast mild and wet, but the coastal

ranges limit this moderating impact to British Columbia's fringe of islands and inlets. Moisture that is not lost over the Cordillera is carried east across the continent by prevailing westerly winds. A rain shadow in the lee of the high Rockies sustains a dry climate in southern Alberta and Saskatchewan, but this effect breaks down as moisture is refurbished across central Canada to insure a humid continental climate for virtually all the east. The most severe maritime effect on the Atlantic coast results in the subarctic impact of Labrador current on Newfoundland's coasts.

In Canada, vegetation responds to soil conditions, which differ with physiography, but is constrained most by climate. Vegetation regions (figure 3) comprise distributions of tundra, grassland, forest and parkland. *Tundra*, characterized by grasses, mosses, sedges and other sub-arboreal species, predominates throughout the Arctic and on Cordilleran ridges. Different arboreal or tree species dominate the changing bands of forest composition south from the tree line to the grassland and Great Lakes. Major forest divisions are the *Subarctic* mixture of deciduous and coniferous scrub, the *Boreal* region of endless conifer, the *Great Lakes Forest* of larger pine and hardwoods and the pre-

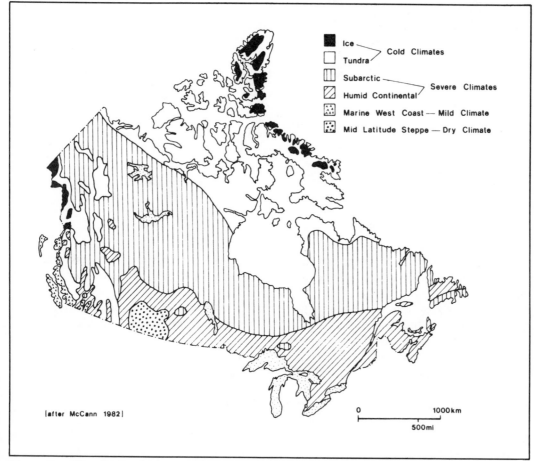

Figure 2. Climatic Regions

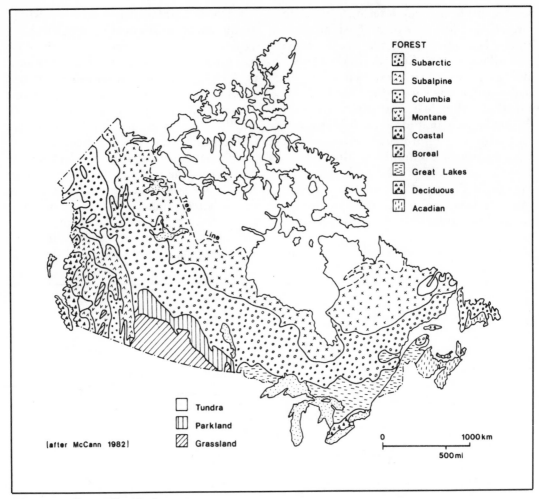

Figure 3.   Vegetation Regions

dominantly *Deciduous* woods of Southern
Ontario. An *Acadian* forest of spruce, pine
and deciduous species is found throughout Maritime Canada, whereas higher Cordilleran ranges in the west show altitudi-
nal bands of stunted subalpine conifers
above *Montane* forests of fir, pine, and
spruce. The *Columbia* forest has species
better suited to drier intermontane conditions and the *Coast* forest boasts massive
cedars, firs and spruces, which benefit
from the greatest rainfall in Canada. Finally, in the Great Plains, *Grasslands* extend from the south to merge into a transi-

tional band of *Parkland* characterized by
isolated strands of aspen to the boreal forest margin.
   Juxtaposition of generally horizontal
vegetation and climate bands across the
vertical trend of landforms distinguishes
Canadian south from north, the established and occupied Canadian provinces
from the distant and unknown territories.
Charter members of Canadian Confederation are the eastern Maritime provinces of
Prince Edward Island, New Brunswick
and Nova Scotia, Quebec, and Ontario (figure 4). Manitoba and British Columbia en-

tered soon after, followed by Alberta and Saskatchewan in 1905. The Yukon Territory was formed in 1898 and the Northwest Territories of Mackenzie, Keewatin and Franklin in 1912. Newfoundland left the British colonial sphere in 1949 to become Canada's tenth province. Sets of provinces and territories define a general scheme of regions, which summarize physical and political boundaries: *Atlantic Canada* is comprised of the Maritime provinces and Newfoundland; Quebec and Ontario lowlands are *Canadian Heartland;* the sparsely populated northern portions of Quebec through Saskatchewan form *Shield Can-*

ada; the Great Plains wedge extending from southern Manitoba to all of Alberta is known as the *Prairies; British Columbia* predominates the Cordillera; and the territories comprise the *Northland.*

SETTLEMENT ON THE MARGINS OF A NORTHERN LAND

Each region displays settlement patterns distinct in form and evolution. Forms are readily distinguished on a map of Canada's settlement zones and range from large blocks of continuous occupation along the boundary with the United States to north-

Figure 4.   Confederated Canada

ern expanses that remain largely uninhabited (figure 3). Territory where neighbors live next to each other in organized
and productive use of land is termed *ecumene* or contiguously occupied territory.
Atlantic Canada's ecumene is mainly
coastal — isolated portions in Newfoundland and fringes along shores of
Nova Scotia, Prince Edward Island, New
Brunswick and Quebec's Gaspé Peninsula.
In New Brunswick and along the Gulf of St.
Lawrence, linear ecumene extends from
the coast up major river valleys like the St.
John and Saguenay. Southern Ontario and
the St. Lawrence Valley blocks comprise
the heartland. Adjacent Shield settlement
reflects discontinuity of habitat and the
dispersed nature of resource development
— Sudbury's mine communities, Temiska-
ming "Clay Belt" farm concentrations and
Chicoutimi's forest industry center.
Throughout the lower Canadian Shield,
ecumene segments are connected by road
and railway to industrial heartland but
remain settlements removed in a resource
hinterland. They provide little continuity
between the heartland and the large block
of agricultural settlement in the Prairies.
And this ecumene contrasts sharply with
the linear settlement in Cordilleran valleys, the mill towns and fishing ports along
the indented British Columbia coast, the
more discontinuous habitation in the
western subarctic hinterland, and the isolated point settlements in the far north.
Point forms may be truly isolated administrative centers like Inuvik in the Northwest Territories, rail-linked mine towns
like Schefferville in Quebec, or temporary
settlements of nomadic natives and resource extraction companies.

All forms of ecumene represent different
legacies of Canadian development as well
as regional adjustments to the land. Canada's historical geography subsequent to
European discovery and penetration is essentially a regional interpretation of the

settlement and development.[6]

Established as fur-trading ventures, 17th
century French colonies on the lower St.
Lawrence and the Bay of Fundy accepted
immigrants and grew as distinct agricultural settlements. On the St. Lawrence, the larger colony, Canada, spread
along both shores of the river between
Montreal and Quebec; on the Bay of
Fundy, Acadia's growth was limited by the
extent that tidal marshland could be diked.
Acadians became expert marshland farmers who grew mainly wheat and peas on
drained fields wrested from the sea with
dike systems and sluice gates. Successful
collective agriculture, which also included extensive animal husbandry and
some fruit and vegetable horticulture, produced a surplus traded to New England in
return for manufactured goods. Coastal
hamlets sustained these and the fur trade
links, and by the end of the French regime
established a distinct rural settlement pattern in the Maritimes. French immigrants
to Canada coming at this time from the
same northwestern parts of France as the
Acadians, found life more ordered and
controlled, first by the Company of New
France and then by administrators of the
crown colony and the Catholic church.
The traditional seigneurial system of land
allocation, similar to the feudal manor system, transferred from France took firmer
hold here than in Acadia and was adapted
by habitants to narrow St. Lawrence river
lowlands through a system of parallel, long
lots stretching back from the shore and
contained in ranges within the *seigneurie*.
Settlement extended along the river and in
successive ranges from it to form parallel
but straggling lines of farmhouses. These
were not villages, for early settlers prized
isolation from authority and equal access

_____

[6]Although now ten years in print, the text for Canada's
historical geography remains R. Cole Harris and John Warkentin, *Canada Before Confederation* (New York: Oxford,
1974).

to land and river resources. By mid-18th century, the end of the French regime, nucleated settlements were more prevalent in the expanding agricultural landscape of the St. Lawrence valley. After the British takeover of Canada in 1763, this rural landscape of farm, village and parish remained and became the refuge for traditional French Canadian society. Population expanded dramatically, agriculture was extended beyond Shield and Appalachian margins, and the exodus to cities and western lands began.

After the conquest, Britain brought its own settlers to Canada — Loyalist refugees from the American Revolution, soldiers who fought for Britain in North America and the displaced from Europe. They were immediately joined or even preceded by U.S. residents who saw settlement opportunity and available land first in the farms of the deported Acadians and later in the newly surveyed townships across the border from New England to the tip of southwestern Ontario. In Ontario, settlement was initiated along the shores of Lake Ontario and Lake Erie, extended by military roads inland and pushed throughout the Ontario peninsula into the Shield. But agricultural settlement in the Canadian Shield proved too marginal and was retracted. During the 19th century the Great Lakes lowland was sown in wheat, then adjusted to mixed farming. Towns were quick to emerge in the agricultural landscape. By mid-century Ontario embarked on its way to leadership in Canadian manufacturing as an extension of the northeastern industrial complex. Linked with emerging industrial towns in the province of Quebec and with Canada's original urban centers, Montreal and Quebec, the Canadian heartland asserted its role as the country's broker. Canada's population and financial base was established and was in search of opportunities for development.

In the late 19th century this goal was realized with construction of a transcontinental railway to open the Prairies to settlement, link British Columbia to the rest of Canada, and keep the Maritimes tied to the emerging heartland economy. With the transfer of the vast Hudson's Bay Company lands to the new nation in 1869, the western interior saw an immediate influx of settlers from eastern Canada and the midwestern United States. When the railroad was completed, they were joined by immigrants who added a new stamp to the Canadian settlement pattern. Among the newcomers were Ukrainians who transferred traditional building techniques and German Mennonites who re-arranged the sectional survey to accommodate nuclear villages and communal farming. With the extension of railroad spurs and roads, Canada's largest block of settlement spread to the rock of Cordillera and Shield, and as far north as killing frosts allowed wheat to grow. In time, settlement was adjusted to land capability: smaller farms in fertile southern Manitoba, expansive wheat farms in Saskatchewan and Alberta, and cattle ranches in the semi-arid southwest quarter of the Prairies.

The strands of ecumene in the Cordillera, which originated with fur trading posts and trails in the region, reflect the extent of habitable river valleys. Forts were succeeded by gold rush towns and provisioning centers along roads, and steamboat runs were established to connect British Columbia's new centers of wealth to the coast. Already the largest population centers in the province at Confederation, Victoria, Nanaimo and lower mainland settlements grew with the rise of lumbering and fishing along the coast. Linking up with the transcontinental railway in the 1880s insured Vancouver's preeminence at the western terminus. By the turn of the century, linear settlement extended along major valleys in the Cordillera and north-

west to Prince Rupert, whereas sawmills
and fish canneries became centers for
point settlements along British Columbia's
rugged coast.

When Canada's Northland was surveyed
and explored in the early 20th century,
point settlements were established as administrative centers for the vast Arctic
land. These joined isolated mining towns
in the Yukon and missions to the Inuit in
the Northwest Territories to produce a far-
flung distribution of tiny settlements in a
largely uninhabited land. Not until after
World War II was this pattern augmented

with carefully spaced defense installations
and weather stations.

Once set, the pattern of settlement remained (figure 5). Migration in Canada
occurred between areas of established
ecumene: people left Atlantic Canada for
southern Ontario and the west, farmers
moved from the heartland to the prairies,
and disillusioned farmers left the prairies
for the west coast or the heartland. Early in
the 20th century most of Canada's arable
land was taken, and migration occurred to
new settlement frontiers in forest and mine
communities of resource hinterlands. But

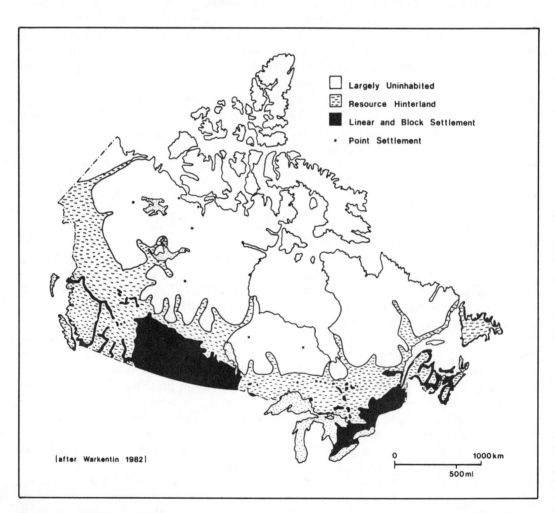

Figure 5.   Settlement Zones

this migration was limited when compared to the move to cities that characterizes Canada's 20th century.

URBAN CANADA

From its earliest settlement, Canada was dominated by urban elements — Montreal and Quebec in New France; Kingston, Toronto and Ottawa in Ontario; Saint John, Halifax and St. John's in Atlantic Canada; Winnipeg in the Prairies; and Victoria in British Columbia. With Confederation, completion of the transcontinental railway and protectionist tariffs, these more populous sections became part of a Canadian urban system, which gained spurts of growth from prairie settlement and wheat production, development of a domestic market for Canadian goods, expansion of manufacturing, concentration of the urban-industrial heartland, wartime production booms, and labor force decline in primary activities like agriculture and forestry.[7] Export of staples has decreased in importance as a mechanism for inducing urban growth. Major cities in Canada have been able to sustain their own growth; by 1976, urban centers were home to 76 percent of the population.

Almost one-third of Canada's people live in metropolitan Toronto, Montreal and Vancouver (figure 6). An additional 25 percent reside in medium-sized metropolitan centers from Victoria to St. John's, and the balance of urban dwellers occupy smaller cities and towns with 1000 or more inhabitants. The distribution of cities reveals urban-industrial regions and development corridors: the *Georgia Strait urban region* focused on Vancouver; the *Albertan Development corridor* from Edmonton

south through Calgary, Lethbridge and Medicine Hat; the *Windsor to Quebec City axis;* and the *Atlantic region urban industrial core* of Saint John, Halifax, St. John's and surrounding areas tied by sea and land.

More important to understanding the urban system is recognition of the hierarchy that prevails among Canadian cities. Toronto and Montreal dominate as primate cities, Toronto as the financial and service center for much of the Canadian hinterland, and Montreal as Canada's eastern entry point and French-Canadian metropolis. Vancouver, although half the size of these eastern giants, is the country's western trade terminus and service center. Of lower order in importance are regional centers like Edmonton, Winnipeg, London, Halifax and Quebec, and industrial cities like Hamilton and Calgary. A third tier in the hierarchy includes cities of over 100,000 population of primary importance in a development corridor but not dominant in their region: Sudbury, Windsor, Victoria, Regina, Saint John, Sherbrooke and others. Below this level, cities have fewer than 100,000 people and comprise distinct orders of places within regional systems. Intermetropolitan linkages of trade, finance, communication and migration are strongest between Toronto and Montreal, and between these primate cities and metropolitan centers just below them in the hierarchy. Whereas the primate cities maintain links with virtually all centers in the subsequent level, links are not well established among cities in this tier. Although Halifax and Winnipeg may not have strong ties, each serves as the regional center for links with the subsequent tier; Regina and Saskatoon are tied to Winnipeg, and Saint John and St. John's connect with Halifax. This system prevails to the lowest levels of the Canadian urban hierarchy and provides the conduits necessary for materials and information to

[7]An overview of the evolution of urban Canada is found in Richard E. Preston, "The Evolution of Urban Canada: The Post-1867 Period," in Robert M. Irving, ed., *Readings in Canadian Geography*, 3rd ed. (Toronto: Holt, Rinehart & Winston, 1978), 19–46. For a readable introduction to Canada's cities see James and Robert Simmons, *Urban Canada*, 2nd ed. (Toronto: Copp Clark, 1974).

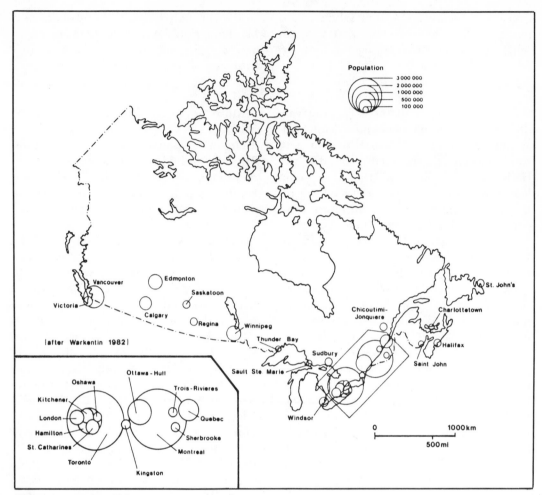

Figure 6.   Major Cities, 1976

flow elsewhere, and for goods, services and directives to reach communities throughout the country.

Recent interregional migration in Canada provides an illustration of the hierarchy in operation. Because of their size and greater range of opportunity, the largest metropolitan centers — Toronto, Montreal and Vancouver — attract and generate the largest number of migrants. The next to greatest migration flows occur between these centers and cities with which they are linked in the subsequent level of the hierarchy. For example, Toron-to sends and receives migrants from Halifax, Winnipeg, Calgary and other second tier centers. Calgary in turn sends and receives migrants from Lethbridge and Red Deer and also from Regina and Saskatoon. In recent years Calgary's growth has exceeded Winnipeg's, and although the Saskatchewan cities are traditionally linked to Winnipeg in the hierarchy, their migrants have gone directly to the Albertan centers of Calgary and Edmonton. Similarly, migrants from St. John's, Newfoundland, bypass the regional center of Halifax on their way to Toronto. The Canadian urban hierarchy is a dynamic system in which flows of goods, migrants and information sometimes act differently or change paths.

Metropolitan dominance is asserted in the hierarchy and in territorial spheres of influence. Currently Toronto dominates the financial and technological decisions that impact on most of Canada; Montreal influences the country east of the Ontario border; and Vancouver's sphere extends into the Prairie provinces. The Windsor-to-Quebec-City axis is a good illustration of the considerable urban growth associated with metropolitan centers. Along "Main Street" Canada, and in line with the nation's two largest cities, are eleven other major urban centers and many smaller ones constituting Canada's only potential megalopolis. Predictions of eventual urban coalescence between Windsor and Quebec project continued growth for Toronto and Montreal,[8] but the growth rates of larger metropolitan areas are slowing, and medium-sized cities such as Victoria, Calgary, Kitchener and Sherbrooke are increasing their pace for a potentially more balanced urban pattern.

Canada's urban landscapes vary considerably from one city to the next and from region to region across the country. Each city's form and growth patterns are constrained by physical features and influenced by urban functions, age, and transportation as well as place in the hierarchy. Hinterland resource extraction centers in the Shield and Cordillera are often company towns, like Kitimat on British Columbia's coast and Terrance Bay on Lake Superior, which display the predetermined geometry, company housing and single industry characteristics of such places. The main streets of service towns in agricultural areas are lined with the commercial, financial and transportation operations required by farmers in the sur-

rounding area, and the side streets with homes occupied by service employees and retired farmers. Larger metropolitan centers are more complex in organization and show more variation in urban character. Each of the major cities identified on figure 6 has an individual character of setting, community patterns, housing and streetscapes, yet all share some of the basic characteristics of large cities and distinguishing marks of Canadian urban places. Well-defined central business districts, flagged as Canadian by the towers of Canadian chartered banks, national hotels and major Canadian department stores, remain viable in the larger centers. Each city maintains clearly defined ethnic sectors sustained by internal mechanisms for upward mobility and a pride of community. Canadian cities are characteristically places where housing is valued, maintained and refurbished; governments at all levels play a significant role in planning; and the urban fabric is well ordered and accessible.

MOVING CANADA'S RESOURCES

The recurring Canadian dilemma of moving resources great distances over terrains varying from an extensive hinterland to a limited heartland or even out of the country has required considerable effort in the development of transportation. All the staples of Canada's economy have needed costly initiatives to retrieve the resources and transfer them for processing and export. Before nationhood, long sea journeys were customary to catch eastern Canada's fish for Europe, and canoe trips and portages from Montreal and Hudson Bay into the heart of the continent were necessary to acquire furs. Subsequent staples — wheat from the western interior, wood and minerals from the Shield and the Cordillera, hydroelectric energy from distant natural or constructed reservoirs, and oil from

[8]Maurice Yeates, *Main Street: Windsor to Quebec City* (Toronto: Macmillan, 1975).

Alberta and the Arctic — all demanded extensive and expensive transportation developments.

After early 19th century canal building to make the Great Lakes more serviceable, attention was diverted to railway construction. In 1876 the Intercolonial Railway linked the isolated Maritimes to Montreal. In 1885 the Canadian Pacific Railway accomplished a transcontinental bond, which served first to carry western wheat to the heartland and to export points at Montreal and later to Vancouver (figure 7). A parallel northern route was subsequently built to convey the produce of

Prairie agriculture as well as minerals from the Shield. Throughout the 20th century, railway spurs were extended northward to transport iron ore from Schefferville in Quebec, base metals from Thompson in Manitoba, and forest products from Prince George in British Columbia. Links with the Northland extend to Moosonee on James Bay, Churchill on Hudson Bay and Great Slave Lake at the southern terminus of the Mackenzie River waterway.

Whereas the Mackenzie is an under-utilized waterway with a brief summer season, the St. Lawrence Seaway connection from the Great Lakes to the At-

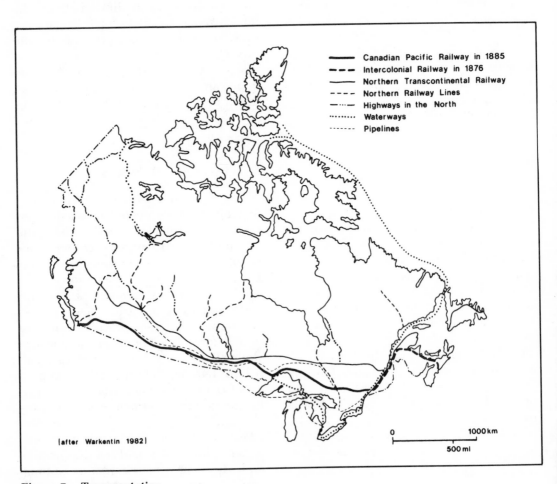

Figure 7.   **Transportation**

lantic is a major route shared by Canada and the United States. For Canada it enables foreign access to Prairie grain and Shield wood products as well as domestic transfers of bulk ores to heartland manufacturing cities. Summer navigation is possible to the high Arctic to provision military and scientific outposts and native settlements.

North of the Canadian National Railway's transcontinental line, highways are the resource links rather than the interurban networks found in Canada's ecumene. The strategic Alaska Highway corrider also serves to funnel natural gas and Yukon minerals south; roads in the area of Great Slave Lake connect mines to the railhead at Hay River. In northwestern Quebec, the massive James Bay hydroelectric development is now connected to the Canadian National Railway and Clay Belt roadways. Paralleling the roads and railways across Canada, pipelines for oil and natural gas carry the valuable fuel from energy-rich Alberta and the Northland to the heartland.

ENVIRONMENTAL CONCERN

Extraction, processing and transfer of resources in Canada have brought with them irreversible environmental change and the spectre of land and resource depletion. Production of staples, whether furs in previous centuries or minerals in recent decades, has exacted a considerable toll from the land. Before the west was settled, many species of fur-bearing animals had already been depleted. Back in Ontario, years of wheat growing brought massive soil erosion before Confederation. In the 20th century, with expansion of the quest for resources into the considerably more fragile environments of Canadian Shield and Arctic tundra, the environmental impact has proved even more sudden and lasting. Mining and smelting in Sudbury created an alien landscape of slag

heaps; emissions from smelters altered vegetation downwind as well as in the settled area. Where Arctic exploration for oil and other minerals was attempted, tracks of machinery remain stamped on the land, and the delicate ecosystems stand threatened with little hope for recovery if they are disrupted. A pipeline raised above ground to save it from the wrenching annual cycle of permafrost could create a barrier to disrupt migration of caribou and other tundra inhabitants.

In southern Canada, where the nation shares a common environment with the United States, the pressures of population and industry are of more immediate concern. Furthermore, the actions in one country often have direct environmental implications for the other. With substantial investment in coal-fired generating plants and the need for inexpensive power, the industrial midwestern and northeastern United States opposes restrictions on emissions that could curb the recently identified devastation of acid rain. As major recipients of this impact that destroys life in lakes and alters vegetation, Canadians from Ontario to Newfoundland are vigorously campaigning in Canada, the United States and international forums to stop acid rain. Cooperative measures were adopted to clean the Great Lakes of destructive effluent. This measure of success plus cross-border agreements to control air and water quality at specific points show promise for resolution of confrontations over joint fishery management and acid rain. With growing United States demand for water, energy and other resources plentiful in Canada, it is particularly imperative for Canadians to establish guidelines for sustained resource use and wise environmental management. For the Canadian environment of wild areas, rural landscapes, industrial land and urban places, this will require definition of priorities in a program of environmental

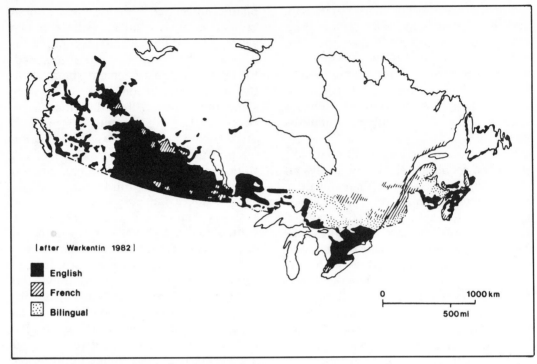

Figure 8.   English and French Language Areas

management.[9] More effort is necessary to save representative wilderness and to assess the seemingly abundant water resources; use of rural land in all its facets is required to insure food supplies and the country life option; industrial land use needs more careful attention to landscape, location, human ecology, zoning, legislation and recycling; and urban spaces could benefit from more attention to diversity, repair of facilities, efficiency and amenity.

LANDSCAPE AND CANADA'S NATIONAL IDENTITY

In the Canadian archipelago of settlement, culture and economic activity, con-

sensus is rarely achieved. Each region remains distinct, with strong symbols of regional identity that emphasize and sustain aspirations and an established way of life. In Quebec, unilingual French and the resurgence of traditional building facades announce regional identity; in Canada's Northland, native expression through resurrected arts compensate for the loss of traditional livelihoods. Differing regional and national policies of resource use have led provinces and the federal government to confrontation. Disagreement between Ottawa and Edmonton on energy policy generated distrust on other federal-provincial issues. This feeling is symbolized by the juxtaposition of well-identified grain carriers on western trains — the bright red cars of the Canada Wheat Board contrast with the blue cars of the Alberta Heritage Fund.

[9]Pierre Danserau, "Problems and Priorities in the Canadian Environment," in *Readings in Canadian Geography*, 258–268.

Yet regional definition in Canada is not necessarily as strong as its symbols. A current map of English and French language areas shows enclaves of French and bilingual population in the western interior, Ontario and the Maritimes, and of English in Quebec (figure 8). Images of French Quebec isolated in English Canada are challenged by the established French enclaves and growing bilingual areas throughout Canada. New Brunswick proclaims itself Canada's truly bilingual province.

The face that Canada turns toward the United States has changed. Once based on a northern identity and expressed through landscape images of caribou, Eskimo and Mountie on frozen tundra, it has become a complex of regional identities difficult to align or simplify in a coherent image. The Canadian condition is a paradox of strong regionalism and strong nationalism. It is a country where geography displays urban enclaves in the wilderness, French farms beside English, traditional fishing next to tidal power generators and oil derricks near Eskimo villages. In a future of integrated economies and increased dependency on external resources, the United States cannot help but look more closely at Canada and try to understand the geography of its neighbor.

Bibliography

Bird, J. B. *The Natural Landscapes of Canada.* Toronto: Wiley, 1972.

Garreau, Joel. *The Nine Nations of North America.* Boston: Houghton Mifflin, 1981.

Gentilcore, R. Louis, ed. *Canada's Changing Geography.* Scarborough, Ont.: Prentice-Hall, Canada, 1967.

Hamelin, Louis-Edmond. *Canada, A Geographical Perspective.* Toronto: Wiley, 1973.

Harris, R. Cole, and John Warkentin. *Canada Before Confederation.* New York: Oxford, 1974.

Irving, Robert M., ed. *Readings in Canadian Geography,* 3rd ed. Toronto: Holt, Rinehart & Winston, 1978.

McBoyle, G. R., and E. Sommerville, eds. *Canada's Natural Environment: Essays in Applied Geography.* Toronto: Methuen, 1976.

McCann, L. D., ed. *A Geography of Canada: Heartland and Hinterland.* Scarborough, Ont.: Prentice-Hall, Canada, 1982.

Metcalfe, William, ed. *Understanding Canada.* New York: New York University Press, 1982.

Putnam, D. F., and R. G. Putnam. *Canada: A Regional Analysis.* Toronto: J. M. Dent and Sons, 1979.

Robinson, J. L. *Concepts and Themes in the Regional Geography of Canada.* Vancouver: Talonbooks, 1983.

Thoman, Richard S. *The United States and Canada, Present and Future.* Toronto: Merrill, 1978.

Warkentin, J., ed. *Canada: A Geographical Interpretation.* Toronto: Methuen, 1968.

Student Activities

The purpose of Konrad's article is to provide the reader with a broad geographic perspective on Canada, one that illustrates how certain phenomena create new emerging regional identities that clash with burgeoning nationalistic impulses. For example, the tundra is characterized by grasses, mosses and other sub-arboreal species and, due to its northern position, spends more time frozen than thawed. These conditions preclude settlements of any magnitude. Strategies recommended for use by secondary students while examining Canada within its changing geographic context follow.

1. Can You Explain?

Often geographers use dramatic phrases to illustrate how geographic phenomena affect the lives of people. Select four of the following descriptions by Konrad and explain each in your own words. Then select one of the four that seems most dramatic to you. Express its meaning through another art form — a poem, segment of a music score, line drawing, or water color.

Few Canadians have ventured to the Arctic archipelago of remnant continental glaciation, seen the tundra that annually breeds the western hemisphere's migratory flocks, experienced summer's constant daylight north of 60°, or stayed to winter the grim Canadian Shield. Yet all are touched by a geography differentiated from that of the United States by its northern characteristics, insularity, and dependency.

A different distance of granite shield and interminable black spruce insures tenous links with Canada's most expansive block of agricultural settlement. As in the Great Plains south of the border, the sectional survey extends linked farms from the forest fringing the Shield in eastern Manitoba to the Rocky Mountain wall in western Alberta. The Rockies and successive parallel ridges

extend to the ocean, isolating valley communities from each other and maintaining a distinct center of blended California culture and British remnants on Canada's Pacific slope.

Canada's physical environment continues to provide the basis for differentiating major regions of the country. Boundaries of natural landscape zones remain distinct after centuries of human attempts to ameliorate differences among them.

Juxtaposition of generally horizontal vegetation and climate bands across the vertical trend of landforms distinguishes Canadian south from north, the established and occupied Canadian provinces from the distant and unknown territories.

When Canada's Northland was surveyed and explored in the early 20th century, point settlements were established as administrative centers for the vast Arctic land. These joined isolated mining towns in the Yukon and missions in the Inuit in the Northwest Territories to produce a far-flung distribution of tiny settlements in a largely uninhabited land.

Canada's urban landscapes vary considerably from one city to the next and from region to region across the country. Each city's form and growth patterns are constrained by physical features and influenced by urban functions, age and transportation, as well as place in the hierarchy.

Hinterland resource extraction centers in the Shield and Cordillera are often company towns, like Kitimat on British Columbia's coast and Terrace Bay on Lake Superior, which display the predetermined geometry, company housing and single industry characteristics of such places.

2. Is It Regionalism or Nationalism?

Canada is often described as a country of paradoxes. One example is the conflict between the regional and national views of Canadians. Use as many sources as you can find to analyze this paradox. Cite your sources for each example and be ready to discuss your findings.

Describe regionalism _____
   Specific examples:
   • Unilingual French
     Source of data   (Article)

Describe nationalism _____
   Specific examples:
   • Canada flag
     Source of data   (Canada handbook)

3. Take a Position!

Konrad states in his article that "In spite of Canadian attempts to establish a separate identity, the country remains strongly influenced by U.S. mass culture as well as economic control." Do you agree or disagree with this statement? Take a position and *in writing* defend it. Provide sufficient evidence. Cite specific examples to document your response.

4. Using The Maps

Study the map entitled "Physiographic Regions" (figure 1). Use this map and other sources as a basis for writing two to four sentences describing each region. Then find a picture from the library or another source that accurately represents each of the divisions. Photocopy it, if necessary. Creatively display your efforts. Find a description of the vegetation of Canada in a library book or other reference. Turn to figure 3. Do your pictures coincide with the descriptions? Given all of this data, where would you expect to find the dense population areas? Mark them in pencil on figure 3. Check your answers with figure 6. If there are discrepancies, how do you account for them? Discuss your responses with your classmates. If you are unable to resolve a discrepancy, check sources on Canadian population patterns.

Finally, carefully review figures 1–7. What patterns do you see? For example, the most heavily populated areas are located on the major Canadian railroad system. (Special Note: Your goal should be to find at least five patterns!)

5. Environmental Management: What Is It? Who Needs It?

Sharpen your research skills by gathering data from a variety of sources that focus on environmental management. In a minimum of three paragraphs describe this idea. Then indicate characteristics of countries that need it. Finally, reflect on Canada's situation and in one or two paragraphs describe why Canada should or should not address this issue.

6. Hinterland or Heartland: Which Do You Prefer?

Imagine for a moment that you were about to be given the choice of living in the heartland or hinterland of Canada for the next ten years. Which would be your choice and why? Write an essay explaining your answer.

CHAPTER 4

Moving Canadian Studies Into the Computer Age

MICHAEL ROESSLER

Informed citizens of the United States and Canada have acknowledged that acid rain constitutes a major threat to the environment of North America. The battle to reduce the emissions that cause it will extend over many years and cost billions of dollars on both sides of the border. What can we social studies teachers do to inform our students about acid rain? How can they best be led to an understanding of the trade-offs involved in such an environmental issue? In addition to the traditional approaches of lectures, discussions and field trips, I suggest having your class design a *computer simulation*. With the infusion of microcomputers into our schools, many students have played computer simulations, but few have had the opportunity to write one. Doing so is a demanding enterprise, but the rewards are commensurate with the efforts.[1]

In the fall of 1982, I worked with a class of 8th graders to produce a computer simulation of this kind with very encouraging results. By working as a class and then in small groups, my students designed their simulation, programmed it in six sections, and then fused them together to make a coherent program. These procedures forced them to use and extend their social, analytical and artistic skills.

I believe that such a project is one of the best potential uses of the microcomputer in the social studies classroom. It deepens the students' understanding of computers and requires them to use higher order cognitive processes of application, analysis, evaluation and synthesis.

A step-by-step description of how a class can create a computer simulation includes nine steps:

1. Perform research
2. Develop a model
3. Determine a scoring mechanism
4. Develop decisions and events
5. Design the structure of the simulation
6. Write a script
7. Program the script
8. Evaluate and revise the program
9. Distribute the program

Although this paper provides guidance

---

[1]The author would like to thank Mary Roessler, Macel Ezell, William Joyce and Martin Batey for reading this manuscript and making many helpful suggestions.

for the creation of a number of computer simulations related to acid rain, the overall process is applicable to hundreds of other topics.

PERFORM RESEARCH

The subject of acid rain, like the pollutants that create it, has few boundaries. In order to research this topic, your students will need to delve into science, economics, law, pressure-group politics, government and international relations. As a beginning, you might ask them to make up a list of descriptors to look up in the card catalog and preliminary sources like *The Readers' Guide to Periodical Literature* and *The Canadian Periodical Index*. While some students use these descriptors to locate relevant books and articles, others should write letters requesting information from the U.S. and Canadian governments, electric power companies and environmental groups. A third group can arrange for guest speakers, films and filmstrips. Two helpful films have been produced by the Canadian Film Board: "Acid Rain: Requiem or Recovery" and "Acid from Heaven." In the United States, these films can be borrowed from the nearest Canadian Consulate without charge.

As these resources become available, your students will need guidance on how to use them. They should begin by taking notes on five major topics:

1. The causes and consequences of acid rain

The importance of this topic is obvious, but your students may need to be reminded that *specific details* are necessary for the simulation. What are the pollutants that create acid rain and where do they come from? When and why did acid rain become a serious problem? What areas are most affected by it? How is an ecosystem affected by precipitation with certain levels of acidity?

2. The contributing actors

In order to construct a simulation, one must also identify the principal actors. As used here, an actor can be an individual, an organization or a group of organizations. For this topic, the list of principal actors includes the polluting industries and their employees, resort owners, environmentalists, Canadian and U.S. government officials, and the general public in both countries. Students should take notes on these actors, their objectives, and their relationships with each other. As they read, they should be on the lookout for pithy quotations that capture different perspectives on the problem of acid rain. These quotes can be woven into the text of the simulation to give it a stronger flavor of realism.

3. Methods of reducing acid rain

During the research process, the students should pay particular attention to alternative ways of combating acid rain and should record notes on all attempts to deal with this problem. They should also note viable solutions that decision makers have overlooked or rejected. A simulation should be an exploration of the real and the possible.

4. Key events

Another helpful way to organize notes on acid rain is to construct a time line of key events, which includes major research findings, conferences, and governmental or industrial decisions. Students can develop individual time lines or produce one jointly. For the latter, staple the skeleton of a time line to your bulletin board and invite your students to flesh it out by adding index cards that include a description of an event, the date it occurred, a footnote on the source, and the name of the student who filled it out. From these events many major sequences of the simulation will be developed.

5. Simulations

In addition to researching acid rain, your

class needs to learn about simulations. If possible, acquire a number of microcomputer simulations and make them available to your students. As they play these simulations, have them take notes on the strengths and weaknesses of each. Also ask them to notice how these simulations are structured and how they move from one decision to another. Eventually, you may want to have your students discuss what makes a good computer simulation.

DEVELOP A MODEL

Simulations are based on models of reality. For example, scientists are currently devising a complex mathematical model to represent the creation and diffusion of acid rain in North America. From this model, they will develop a computer simulation that shows the relationship between the amount of air pollution released in one area and the level of acidity of the precipitation falling on another area. Fortunately, educational simulations need not be based on the sophisticated modeling techniques required for such a simulation. Yet enough of a model should be formulated to identify the key mechanisms at work and the basic assumptions underlying your simulation. When your students do this, they will be forced to isolate the inner workings of acid rain politics and clarify their own understanding of them.

The best models of industrial pollution are based on the economists' concept of *externalities,* which is explained in most basic economics textbooks. It is applied to the problem of acid rain in Irene H. van Lier's excellent book, *Acid Rain and International Law.*[2] As van Lier explains them, externalities represent a failure of the capitalist marketplace. Theoretically, a business should be forced to absorb all of its

own costs and to recover them in the price of its products. One of these costs is dealing with waste by-products. In the case of gaseous wastes like sulfur dioxide and nitric oxides, however, businesses are able to shoot them into the air and let them go where they may. Once in the atmosphere, these gases are mixed with other substances and are blown for hundreds of miles. When they fall to earth in the form of acid precipitation, they generate external (or social) costs by corroding buildings, killing lakes, and stunting the growth of plants and animals. The customers of these businesses are able to enjoy artificially deflated prices because certain costs of production are passed on to communities downwind of the polluting factories.

In a capitalist society, businesses are driven to maximize their profits. Consequently, they can be expected to take advantage of externalities whenever they are allowed to do so. When will a business spend millions of dollars to remove pollutants from its smokestack emissions? Probably only when the government requires it to do so. Since government is usually influenced by its local industries, it will enforce emission controls only when pressured by environmental groups and other concerned citizens.

This analysis has thus far ignored the complication that not just one government is involved here, but several governments. Regulation of industries is a responsibility shared by the federal and provincial governments in Canada and by the federal and state governments in the United States. Furthermore, air pollutants have a nasty way of ignoring international boundaries. Sulfur dioxide and nitric oxides have been flowing in both directions across the U.S.-Canadian border for decades. Consequently, aggrieved citizens are often faced with the problem of trying to move a foreign government to regulate the emissions of its industries. This must

---

[2]Irene H. van Lier, *Acid Rain and International Law* (Toronto: Bunsel Environmental Consultants, 1981), 56–61.

normally be done through negotiations between the two federal governments.

Your students may choose to adopt this model of externalities or to develop a model of their own. Then they will have to decide from whose point of view their simulation will be written. There are at least four distinct possibilities:

VIEWPOINT	RESULTING FOCUS
Environmentalists	How can a citizen group initiate policy in a democracy?
Industries	How do industries make decisions about pollution control?
U.S. president	What can a president do to reduce acid rain?
Canadian prime minister	What can a prime minister do to reduce acid rain?

An effective simulation can be created from each of these four vantage points. In fact, it is desirable to have one from each and to let students explore the problem of acid rain from these different viewpoints.

I am focusing on the Canadian prime minister and describing how a simulation can be designed from his or her point of view, because I believe that a successful resolution of the acid rain problem will probably have to be initiated in Ottawa. A first-rate simulation of the prime minister's situation might suggest how this task can be accomplished.

Because of the prevailing wind patterns, Canada receives more air pollutants from the U.S. than it gives in return. Canadians also have more cause for alarm, because two of their major industries are threatened by acid rain — tourism and forestry. Thus, it is reasonable to base a simulation on the assumption that the Canadian prime minister is motivated strongly (but not solely) to eliminate the problem of acid rain. The channels that this official must follow in doing so are represented in figure

1. The prime minister must work through several intermediaries to achieve pollution control. These include the Canadian Parliament, the provincial governments, and the U.S. government. Another approach that has been used by the prime minister is to mobilize public opinion in both Canada and the United States through the production of movies and brochures and the funding of research.

A simulation written from the prime minister's perspective should reflect the channels depicted in figure 1. It should also show the forces influencing her or him to intensify or relax abatement efforts, including the press, the Cabinet, Parliament, affected industries and the Canadian electorate. If the prime minister alienates any of these groups, his or her effectiveness in dealing with acid rain, and maybe even the current government, will be jeopardized.

This section describes a model of acid rain politics as seen from the prime minister's point of view. Your class may devise a very different model, and that is all the better as long as it accurately depicts the

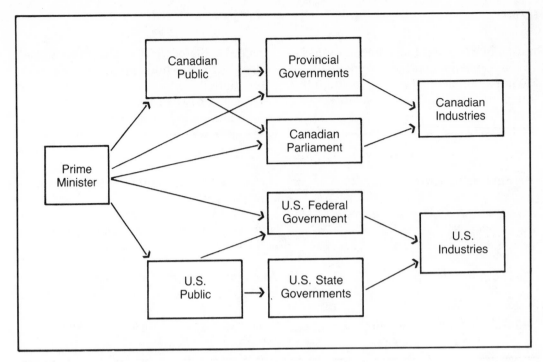

Figure 1. How the Prime Minster Effects Emission Controls

relationships between the major actors in this international political drama.

The simulation will, of course, be based upon whatever model is constructed. Its events, decisions and outcomes should all derive from this model and the assumptions that underlie it. For example, if the player/prime minister presses too hard for the control of emissions from Canadian sources, the program should produce a strong reaction from the affected industries and representatives favorable to them in the provincial and federal governments.

DETERMINE A SCORING MECHANISM

One of the primary appeals of a computer simulation is its competitive aspect. Students enjoy the challenge of competing against each other or against a norm established by the computer. A scoring system helps focus attention on the objectives of

the simulation, and so it should be chosen carefully.

The simulation described here assumes a major objective of the prime minister to be the curtailment of acid rain. A second primary objective would be the preservation of the existing government. These two objectives can be used in devising a scoring system for the simulation. Of course, each of them will have to be objectified in a measure that can be raised or lowered as the game proceeds.

For the level of acid rain, we can use the total estimated amount of sulfur dioxide and nitric oxide gases emitted annually by the United States and Canada combined. A successful player will be able to reduce these emissions and thereby reduce the amount of acid rain. An unsuccessful player will be unable to stop the natural increase of the emission levels expected to accompany the growth of the Canadian and U.S. economies. The beginning levels of these pollutants and the increments or decrements that occur in the game should approximate their levels in the real world. The program can begin by using the emission levels of 1978 as base figures — 33.5 million tons of sulfur dioxide and 26.1 million tons of nitric oxides.[3]

To quantify the other objective — the prime minister's ability to stay in office — either of two measures can be used. The most closely related measure is his or her support in Parliament. When that support falters, the prime minister must resign or call for new elections. If a general election is called for, the final decision between the prime minister and the opposition will be made by the electorate. This process suggests a second possible measure — the percentage of the electorate that supports the prime minister. I believe that the structure of Canada's government makes this level of popular support an excellent

choice for the simulation's scoring system. Prime ministers who alienate a large percentage of the voters are not destined to remain in office for long. This measure will be simpler to present and will be more readily understood by those students who are not familiar with Canada's parliamentary system.

By using these two measures — emission levels of acidic pollutants and the percentage of popular support for the prime minister — we can design an effective scoring system for our simulation. Within the program, there should be a scoring page (see figure 2) that is called up periodically to inform the player of his or her progress.

---

[3]The breakdown by source country was as follows:

	U.S.	Canada
sulfur dioxide	28 million tons	5.5 million tons
nitric oxides	24 million tons	2.1 million tons

Ross Howard and Michael Perley, *Acid Rain: The Devastating Impact on North America* (New York: McGraw-Hill Book Co., 1982), 43–47.

CURRENT SCORE

Prime Minister's Popularity 62%

Emissions Level

Beginning ██████████████████████████████ 50 million tons

Current ███████████████████████████ 45 million tons

* *
*   Keep popularity above 40%   *
* *

Figure 2.   A Sample Scoring Page

As the game proceeds, the outcomes of certain events and decisions will produce changes in the players' scores. The program might, for example, make responses like these:

Great news! Cornplanters' Power Company has agreed to install scrubbers in all five of its generating plants. This will eliminate 300,000 tons of sulfur dioxide emissions per year.

Too bad. The government's pollution control requirements have raised the price of automobiles and angered the consumers. Your popularity has fallen by 5%.

To continue playing the game, a player should be required to maintain a certain level of popular support. Otherwise, her or his government will fall and, along with it, the opportunity to reduce acid rain.

The goals of the game will be defined in terms of whatever scoring system is established. These goals can be absolute ("You must lower emissions to 35 million tons per year") or relative ("Try to beat the best score that has been achieved so far").

DEVELOP DECISIONS AND EVENTS

The next step in designing your simulation is to identify the decisions and events that a player will encounter in the course of the game. For acid rain, as for most subjects, the real world provides a rich source of ideas for the components. Therefore, it is important to have your class develop a time line. A partial time line and description of its use follows as an illustration.

1973   A concerned citizens group sued the International Nickel Company for violating air pollution regulations. The subsequent conviction of INCO embarrassed the Ontario government for its handling of pollution control.

1979   Ontario's Minister of the Environment, Harry Parrott, announced that Ontario's lakes were more acidic than was gen-

erally believed. He said that 48,000 of them could die by the year 2000.

1980   The United States decided to convert 62 New England plants to coal, thereby increasing their emissions by 25%.

The United States and Canada signed a Memorandum of Intent to negotiate a treaty on acid rain.

1981   Prime Minister Trudeau and President Reagan met in Ottawa. Three thousand Canadian protestors confronted the president outside of Parliament waving signs saying *Go Home Acid Rain* and *Save This Fish*.

1982   Canada offered to achieve a 50% reduction in sulfur dioxide emissions by 1990 if the U.S. would reciprocate. The U.S. rejected the offer.

1982   The Canadian government announced that more than $40 million would be spent over the next three years on acid rain research.

Many of these events were beyond the control of the prime minster. They have, however, affected his or her ability to deal with the problem of acid rain. Consequently, they can be incorporated into the simulation as periodic announcements or news bulletins. Here is a sample:

The U.S. president just announced that 62 New England power plants will be allowed to convert to coal. This will result in an *increase* of 300,000 tons of sulfur dioxide emissions per year.

When possible, it is desirable to base the simulation's events on real happenings. It is certainly permissible, though, to spice up the program with a number of history's might-have-beens. A little thought yields several plausible developments:

Quabbin Reservoir becomes contaminated by acid rain and 2 million people in the Boston area are left without water.

An environmentalist is elected president of the United States.

A smelting plant closes in Ontario laying off 1,500 workers. The owners cite pollution control as the main cause of the closing.

Anti-U.S. demonstrations in Canada set back acid rain negotiations by at least two years.

As will be explained in the section on designing the structure of a simulation, an event need not "occur" each time the simulation is played. It can be called up once every three games, once every ten games, or in whatever way the designers decide to use it.

Actions that involved the prime minister, or that could have done so, provide the material for decisions that can be built into the simulation. For example, the last entry in the time line suggests a decision on the allocation of funds available to combat acid rain:

Fifteen million dollars is available each year for the government to use in its fight against acid rain. As prime minister, how would you like the largest share to be spent?

a. Research.
b. Enforcement of emission control laws.
c. Pouring lime into lakes to reduce their acidity.
d. A campaign to inform U.S. citizens about acid rain.

Press the letter of your choice.

This is a decision that can be presented several times during a simulation. Doing so will simplify the programming task and enable the player to adjust her or his strategies as the game progresses.

Even the limited time line presented here suggests a number of other decisions that can form an integral part of your class's simulation. What *quid pro quos* should the player/prime minister offer when negotiating with the United States? Or, how much should he or she pressure Ontario to clamp down on its smelters and power plants? Decisions can also be drawn

from the realm of the possible. Would the player embark on a major program of energy conservation as a means of reducing acid rain? Or would the player commit the Canadian government to pay for the installation of scrubbers in the smokestacks of all plants emitting high levels of sulfur dioxide? By using the time line and their imaginations, your students should be able to compile a long list of similar decisions to be incorporated into their simulation.

How do the game designers select the decisions to include in the simulation? A good decision is realistic and dramatic. It should focus attention on some critical aspects of the dynamic under study and thereby contribute to the objectives of the game. A good decision must also be straightforward enough to be presented in a concise, multiple choice format.

Another important criterion for a good decision is identified by McGuire, Solomon and Bashook in their most useful book *The Construction and Use of Written Simulations.* The authors argue that every decision should allow at least one response choice from each of three categories: those that are harmful to the player's chances of success, those that are helpful and those that are neutral. Selecting decisions that allow this diversity of response will make the game more rewarding by clearly differentiating between successful and unsuccessful strategies.[4]

Once the decisions have been selected and the choices for each identified, the designers must decide how the computer should respond to each of those choices. To illustrate how that process might be carried out, consider the decision on the allocation of federal monies. Here are responses that can be programmed for each of the following four choices:

---

[4]Christine H. McGuire, Lawrence M. Solomon and Philip G. Bashook, *Construction and Use of Written Simulations.* (New York: Harcourt Brace, 1976), 114–5.

CHOICE	RESPONSE
Research	Periodically announce research findings that may or may not help abatement efforts.
Enforcement of emission control laws	Make the effects conditional on whether or not adequate control laws had been established earlier in the game.
Pouring lime into lakes to reduce acidity	Liming has been tried with disappointing results. Make this a dead-end choice.
A campaign to inform U.S. citizens about acid rain	This tactic has been surprisingly effective, but it is risky, Players overrelying on this choice should be confronted with a backlash from the U.S.

As implied by these suggested responses, the writer of a computer simulation has the luxury of choosing from among several possible methods of response. A particular response can be programmed to appear every time a certain decision is made, a given percentage of times, or only when certain conditions are met.

Naturally, most of the computer's responses to decisions made in the game should be reflected in the score. In the sample program described here, that consists of changes in the level of popular support for the prime minister or in the level of acid rain-producing emissions.

DESIGN THE STRUCTURE OF THE SIMULATION

Once your students have identified the events and decisions that they would like to include in the simulation, they can choose the best structure for organizing those elements into a system. To facilitate this process, you might write the decisions and events on index cards so they can be moved around to experiment with different patterns.

In organizing a computer simulation, at least three main kinds of structures can be used: linear, modified linear and branching. Your class can adopt any of the three or a combination of them.[5]

Linear

A linear simulation presents the same items in the same sequence each time it is played. A shortened version of a linear simulation might look like this:

Introduction ——> Decision 1 ——>
Event 1 ——>   Decision 2 ——>
Event 2 ——> End

Linear simulations are the easiest to program, but they suffer from several inherent weaknesses. One is that the route of the program cannot be determined by any of the player's decisions. This limitation rules out the use of many good design strategies. Moreover, linear simulations are not very replayable. The best computer simulations motivate students to play them over and over again, continually presenting them with new situations and allowing them to experiment with different strategies. For these reasons, some use of the other two kinds of structures is recommended.

Modified Linear

The computer's random function allows the designer to adopt an approach that I

---

[5]In this discussion of structures, I am indebted to McGuire et al., Chapter 8.

call modified linear (figure 3). In it, the basic linear structure is retained except that, at certain junctures, the computer chooses from among several options to place in a certain slot (see figure 3).

Each time a program with this structure is played, the computer randomly determines whether to use decision 1a or 1b as the first decision, whether to use event 1c or 1d as the first event, and so on. This modified linear approach is easy for student designers to visualize, yet it makes a simulation much more rewarding to those who play it repeatedly. On the other hand, it requires nearly twice as much programming as a linear design and still does not allow for the degree of player control provided by branching.

Branching

The most effective simulations use considerable branching. Naturally, they are the hardest to design and program. A simplified branching structure is diagrammed in figure 4. Decisions about the program's path can be determined in many ways. Sometimes, it is appropriate to let the player decide which branch he or she would like to follow. At other times, the branching should be determined by certain conditions that occur as the game progresses. If a prime minister were to experience a major disagreement with the Parliament, for example, the program should pursue a branch that simulates a general election in order to determine whether or not the player can retain the office and continue the game.

Having been introduced to these three methods of structuring a simulation, your class (or a designated committee) should proceed to manipulate the cards containing the decisions and events in order to experiment with different structures. Once a satisfactory one has been created, a diagram of it should be drawn up and approved by the class.

Write a Script

Before the actual programming of your simulation is begun, your students should write a script. This task is relatively simple once the decisions and events have been developed and organized into a diagram.

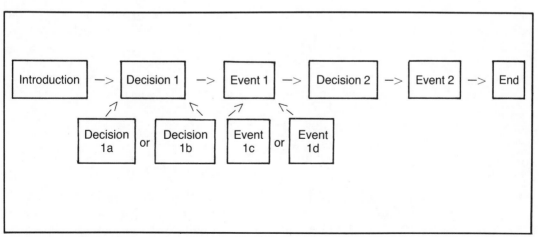

Figure 3.   Modified Linear Approach

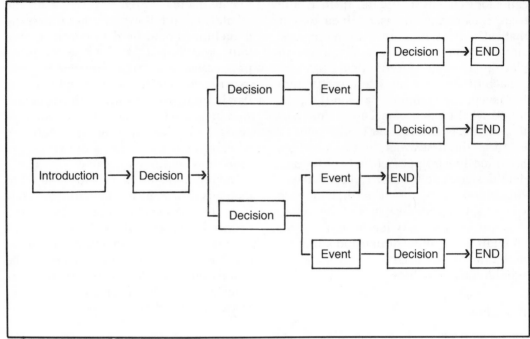

Figure 4.   A Branching Simulation

Script writing should be marked by creative flashes as the writers are forced to visualize what form the actual pages will take and come up with sounds, pictures and perhaps a few good puns that can be incorporated into the program.

You might provide a standard form for the scriptwriters to use. This form should have a column for the text that will be displayed on the screen and also a column for pertinent information required by the programmers: sound, branching instructions, etc.

Scriptwriters should also be given guidelines from which to work. These guidelines should include those appropriate for all written media, plus others specifically applicable to the microcomputer medium:

- The reading level must be appropriate for the intended players.
- The introduction should be brief and clear. Players must become immedi-

ately involved in the simulation.
- Pages should be uncluttered and easy to read. Double spacing is preferred.
- Player inputs must be simple to make, generally restricted to multiple choice and yes/no options.
- Screen formats should be varied as much as possible. Think of creative ways to break up chunks of text and to display them in different locations on the screen.
- The player should be able to control the pace of the movement from one page to another ("Press the space bar to continue").
- Grammar, spelling and punctuation must be correct.
- The program's responses should be consistent and appropriate.

The fate of the simulation depends largely on the quality of the written script. At this point, you may want to make your greatest contributions to the project by offering suggestions, proofreading, and perhaps insisting that certain parts of the script be rewritten before the programming is begun.

One of the main assets of a computer program is that it is actually several media in one. A computer simulation can make use of sound, color graphics and even animation if the programmers have the skill and time to include them.

In planning for graphics, it is important for student scriptwriters to know the capabilities of the computer that the simulation will be programmed on. Most microcomputers can make low-resolution graphics, which allow pictures to be built up by giving colors to small squares on a grid, like a mosaic. Low-resolution graphics are easy to program. For an acid rain simulation, they can be used to add simple images of a factory, a lake or a fish. These graphics add variety and color to the program, but not much information because they lack detail.

Most microcomputers also have a high-resolution graphics capability, which enables the creation of detailed colored maps, graphs and drawings for inclusion in the program. For the simulation, high-resolution graphics can be used to make a map showing those areas of Canada receiving the greatest amount of acid precipitation or a diagram illustrating how acid rain is created.

In addition to requesting graphic displays, the scriptwriters should also designate where sounds might be incorporated into the program. The occasional use of sound gives energy and a sense of realism to a program. Telegrams can be clicked onto the screen; phones can be rung; and simple tunes can be played at dramatic moments. Of course, sound should be used in moderation. The completed simulation should not squawk and squonk like a video game. Also, each player must be able to decide whether to run the simulation with or without sound. Schools often use their computers in places where noisy programs would disrupt the surrounding activities.

PROGRAM THE SCRIPT

The actual programming of a simulation is a slow process that should usually be done outside of class time. It can be turned over to a committee of programmers from your class or perhaps to a computer programming class.

Computer programmers normally break up large assignments into modules that can be programmed separately. These modules can eventually be fused together into a long program or they can be saved on a disk so that the computer moves from module to module as the simulation is run. Programming in modules requires careful planning and coordination, particularly with regard to variables. Some key variables will be used by all the programmers and must be established in advance. Each programmer also needs to have a list of variables that she or he may use exclusively. All programmers should be instructed to keep notes on the location and function of each variable that is introduced.

The graphics displays can be programmed rather easily and can be done by nonprogrammers if the appropriate resources are available. Particularly helpful in this regard are the electronic sketching programs that enable one to make high-resolution pictures by using a joystick or game paddles. I have found that the best way to use these programs is to draw (or trace) the desired pattern on a transparency and then tape it over the screen of the monitor. Programming the graphic then becomes a simple matter of drawing lines electronically under the lines of the transparency. The completed picture can be saved on a disk to await incorporation into the final program.

" . . . however we may have a definite lead on what's causing your hair to rust . . . . "

EVALUATE AND REVISE
THE PROGRAM

Once the simulation has been programmed, the designers should test it.
They need to pay close attention to the
scoring system. How hard is it to win the
game? Do the adjustments to a player's
score seem appropriate for the decisions
and events that elicit them? An ideal simulation is neither too easy nor too frus-
trating. When testing it, the designers
should sometimes use poor strategies,
sometimes good ones, and sometimes a
mixture of the two. Even when the designers try to make all the right decisions, they
ought not to win every time. Both good
strategy and good fortune should be necessary to win.

If time allows, have your students field
test their simulation on a sampling of players. As evaluators, they can observe and
take notes on any parts of the program that
confuse these players. They can also notice
how well the players score on their first,
second and third trials. If the scoring system has been adjusted properly, very few
players will win the first time they play.

DISTRIBUTE THE PROGRAM

Once the simulation is completely debugged, field tested and modified, your students will have an exciting opportunity to share the results with others. I am not aware of a software company that has published a program written by a class, but I think it not unlikely for this to occur. If your class's simulation turns out exceptionally well, you may want to submit it to a publisher for consideration. Most publishers expect to add refinements and conduct further testing before marketing a program. Thus when you submit your students' program, you should include a cover letter describing the improvements that could be made if it were published.

Most student-created simulations will not be of publishable quality, but good enough to share with other schools. To do so, you should place it in the public domain and give copies to various user groups and public domain distribution centers. In this way, copies of your students' simulation will soon be dispersed all across Canada and the United States. This widespread distribution should please your students, providing them the satisfaction of authorship and the knowledge that they have contributed to the fight against acid rain. What better way to end a semester?

Bibliography

Boyle, Robert H. "An American Tragedy." *Sports Illustrated* (September 21, 1981): 68–82.

Howard, Ross, and Michael Perley. *Acid Rain: The Devastating Impact on North America*. New York: McGraw-Hill Book Co., 1982.

McGuire, Christine H., Lawrence M. Solomon, and Philip G. Bashook. *Construction and Use of Written Simulations*. New York: Harcourt Brace, 1976 paperback.

Maidment, Robert, and Russell H. Bronstein. *Simulation Games: Design and Implementation*. Columbus, OH: Charles E. Merrill Publishing Co., 1973.

Punnett, R. M. *The Prime Minister in Canadian Government and Politics*. Toronto: Macmillan of Canada, 1977.

"Simulations and Beyond." *Classroom Computer News* (Jan.-Feb. 1983).

Weller, Phil, and the Waterloo Public Interest Research Group. *Acid Rain: The Silent Crisis*. Kitchener, Ont.: Between The Lines And The Waterloo Public Interest Group, 1980.

Student Activities

A major feature of Roessler's article is a step-by-step presentation of how a social studies class can create and use a computer simulation. It is based on the author's research with a group of 8th graders who designed and programmed a computer simulation addressing the acid rain issue. Such an activity encourages students to use and extend their social, analytical and artistic skills in positive ways. Their understanding of what computers can do requires them to use higher-order thinking skills and serves as a motivator for learning complicated content. The following activities are intended to enhance the development of computer simulations in the classroom.

1. How Much Acid Is in Our Rain?

Ask your science teacher for some pH paper. Exposed to precipitation, pH paper enables you to measure the acidity in the environment in your community. Ideally, you should measure pH immediately after it begins to rain and then at the end of the rainfall. These measurements, taken over an extended period of time, will enable you to gain firsthand knowledge of the fluctuations in the acidity of rainfall in your area. Additional pH tests should be run on nearby rivers and lakes to test for conditions leading to acid shock. Make a chart for reporting your data. What "tentative" conclusions can you draw? Can you make any generalizations? Why? Why not? What new questions are raised by your data?

2. How Can I Start Writing a Simulation?

Select a couple of existing simulations (*Bafa' Bafa'*, or *Explorers I* and *Explorers II*, both published by Simili II, 1150 Silverado, La Jolla, CA 92037). Try to construct flow charts from them. This is a very challenging exercise that can help you come to grips with the concept of branching or webbing. Webbing or branching is a good way to expand your thinking about a certain topic. Look over the branching simulation (figure 4) and the web example (figure 5) to see what webbing or branching is all about.

After you have studied the example, begin analyzing the simulations. What are the central themes? What major ideas support these themes? What descriptors support the main ideas? What ideas spin off from each major idea? What supportive ideas can you think of? What comes to mind when you break down each supporting idea? After completing at least one web, begin thinking about acid rain. If the topic is new to you, do some reading about it. Use the card catalog, *Reader's Guide to Periodical Literature* and the *Canadian Periodical Index*.

When you are ready to construct your web on acid rain, write the topic in the center of the web. Then add all the ideas that relate to the topic to the web. Actually, the more intricate and complex your web is, the more useful it will be and the more challenging your simulation will be. You are now ready to run a pilot of your simulation. Work in pairs; then in small groups critique each other's work.

3. What Tools Will Assist Me in Making Rational Choices About Acid Rain — Or Any Other Social/Political Issue?

Your knowledge of major propaganda techniques will assist you in making informed choices about acid rain or other social issues. The following techniques are among the most commonly used:

● Name calling — consists of labeling an individual or group such as "commu-

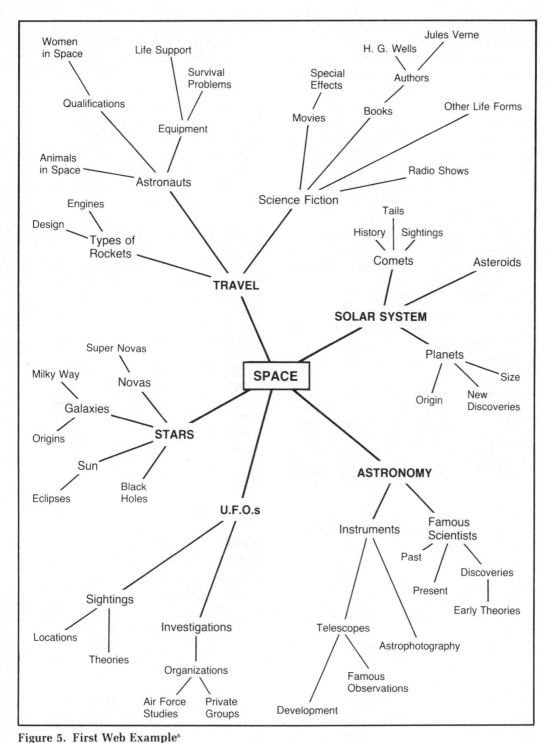

Figure 5. First Web Example[6]

[6]Mary Ann Haley, Charles Parkham, Peg Purdy and Becky Smith Tamlyn. *Independent Research: Student Notebook* (Littleton, MA: IRSN, 1981); 12.

nist," "red-necks," and "trendy environmentalist."

- Glittering generality — used to describe a person or a product in a favorable light and is usually the opposite of name calling, i.e., "honest," "pure," "trustworthy," "modern," or "naturalist."
- Transfer — involves the joining of a symbol or idea toward which the reader has less favorable attitudes with another symbol whose acceptance is more certain: an "innocent" child unable to fish because of toxic waters.
- Testimonial — involves a famous person endorsing an idea or a product, for example, the U.S. president endorsing reduced sulfur emission.
- Cardstacking — involves rigging the facts by concealing certain information or by emphasizing other information. For example, the chart of a company's earnings may be constructed in such a way as to minimize losses over a long period while dividends of the last few years are highlighted. The graph of acid rain in one section of the country may be shown to indicate that there is little problem with acid rain; however, the graph that shows the dramatic contrast experienced by another section of the country is not revealed.
- Plain folks device — here the propagandist is one of us. Examples are a farmer describing how the yield of spinach and lettuce has been significantly reduced by acid rain or a tourist describing how the Lincoln Memorial is suffering from this unnatural erosion.
- Bandwagon procedure — appeals to the group instinct. It urges one to do it because "everyone else is doing it."

Look for these techniques in the media. You can also use this knowledge in your acid rain simulation. Two excellent films, *Acid Rain: Requiem or Recovery* and *Acid from Heaven*, contain prime examples of propaganda plus a wealth of important information. Both are produced by the Canadian Film Board and are available free from the nearest Canadian Consulate. If time allows, compare their contents and propaganda techniques with media obtained from conservation and environmental clubs and from utility companies.

Make a chart listing each of the propaganda techniques. Under each category list specific examples. See how many you can find in three weeks.

4. Can You Win at Acid Rain Scrabble?
Challenge a friend to a game of Scrabble. Add new rules: (1) All words must relate to acid rain and (2) Each term should be defined contextually. Examples are:

acid rain	architectural	nitrogen
aquatic life	structures	ecosystem
manganese	bronchitis	flora
emissions	vapor	buffered
geysers	atmosphere	oxides
marshlands	fauna	alkaline
emphysema	basalt	sulfur
granite	toxic	neutralize
pH	heavy metals	algae
fossil fuel		

5. How Good Are You at Trivial Pursuit?
Design and play a version of Trivial Pursuit focusing on important questions about acid rain. Not only is the game a great culminating activity, but it also can give you experience in writing clear, precise questions focusing on the causes of this problem, effects on the environment, and proposals for elimination of pollution from the atmosphere. It is best to create your questions at the beginning of our study of acid rain. You can begin to revise your questions as you explore this topic in greater detail. Your senator and representative are valuable sources of printed matter about acid rain.

CHAPTER 5

Using Canadian Literature To Understand Canada

WENDY K. SUTTON

Though the use of literature, history and biography by and about Canadians, social studies teachers can guide their students to a fuller understanding of the geographic, historical, cultural, social, economic and political factors that have shaped Canadians as people and Canada as a nation. Although an attempt has been made to label the literature as more appropriate for students in grades 6-9 or in grades 10-12, many of the selections will extend the understanding of a particular topic or concept regardless of the grades in which it is used. Much of the literature accessible to younger students is rich in detail and description and suitable for use with senior students, and often excerpts from more difficult literature can be shared effectively with younger students. Students in grades 6-9 will also benefit from hearing some of the short stories, essays and poems recommended for the older students.

THE LAND

Descriptions of the vastness and wilderness of the land and of the bitterness of the climate fill the journals of the early explorers and settlers of what is now Canada. The lengthy winter and fear of being lost in a hostile environment were major concerns of both explorers and pioneers. Physical or emotional defeat, and even death, often came to those unable to cope with the wilderness and isolation. In *Travels and Adventures in Canada and the Indian Territories between the Years 1760 and 1776*, Alexander Henry describes his fear of the land and of being lost — "unknowing where to go, bewildered, and like a madman." Although thrilled by the spectacular mountains, rivers and sunsets, Susanna Moodie, in her journal *Roughing It in the Bush*, describes her feelings of hopeless imprisonment as she was constantly forced to cope with the disagreeable and often harsh realities of nature: "At that period my love for Canada was a feeling nearly allied to that which the condemned criminal entertains for his cell — his only hope of escape being through the portals of the grave."

Even after 400 years of exploration and settlement in Canada, vast areas remain undeveloped and challenging, and this reality has shaped and found expression in the writing of many Canadian authors and poets. In *The Bush Garden*, valuable also for its Preface introducing the concept of region in both physiographic and cultural terms, Northrup Frye writes: "I have long been impressed in Canadian poetry by a tone of deep terror in regard to nature . . . . It is not a terror of the dangers or discomforts or even the mysteries of nature, but a terror of the soul at something that these things manifest."

In *Survival: A Thematic Guide to Canadian Literature*, Margaret Atwood proposes that the unifying symbol in Canada and in Canadian literature is survival and a preoccupation with the obstacles to survival be they external and physical or internal and spiritual. Although not all Canadian literature depicts nature as unrelenting and hostile, Northrup Frye has also stated that the imminence of nature is central in Canadian writing.

Atwood's *Survival* is a valuable source of descriptions of novels, short stories and poetry that provide historical, cultural and social views of Canada and of specific groups of Canadians. Two anthologies rich with literary material of value to social studies teachers of grades 6-12 are *Skookum Wawa*, edited by Gary Geddes, and *Marked by the Wild: An Anthology of Canadian Literature Shaped by the Canadian Wilderness*, Bruce Littlejohn and Jon Pearce, editors. Through using only literature, there is clearly a danger of presenting a distorted picture of Canada, where, as in the United States, three-quarters of the people live in cities (the majority of Canadians also live within 150 miles of the U.S. border). However, Canadian literature like that cited so far does offer compelling views of many of the forces that have decisively shaped Canadians and Canada.

A resource that will help students grasp the unique characteristics of the geographical regions that comprise Canada is *Profile of a Nation*, edited by Alan Dawe. In this collection are essays such as "Canada's Regions," by Kildare Dobbs, which describe the individual regions in historical and cultural terms, and "A Mosaic of Provinces," by Claude Julien, which does the same thing from a more political stance.

Much literature also describes the specific regions of Canada in greater depth. The Pacific Northwest is the subject of the previously mentioned *Skookum Wawa* and of selections in *Marked by the Wild*. For students in grades 6–9, two novels by Roderick Haig-Brown were inspired by the author's strong feelings for the forests and coastline of British Columbia. *Starbuck Valley Winter* dramatizes the dangers of outdoor life as two boys spend the winter trapping. In *Saltwater Summer* the same boys share the hazards and excitement of commercial fishing. In addition to sharing his deep knowledge and understanding of the Canadian wilderness, Haig-Brown introduces young readers to many unfamiliar activities such as setting traps, skinning a deer, making a waterwheel, trolling and seining.

The sharply distinctive geography of the prairies and its impact upon the people who live there is the subject of the short stories by Sinclair Ross in *The Lamp at Noon and Other Stories*. Also, perhaps more appropriate for older students, is *Who Has Seen the Wind*, by W. O. Mitchell. This novel, set in a small prairie town during the Depression, chronicles the influence of the landscape upon the physical, social and spiritual growth of a young boy. Also set in the prairies during the Depression, two books by the famous Canadian artist William Kurelek would be particularly effective with students in grades 6-9. There are really only two seasons on the prairies, and in *A Prairie Boy's Winter* and *A Prairie Boy's Summer* Kurelek, through story and paintings, memorably describes the chores and games associated with the extreme climatic temperatures of winter and summer.

As for the Pacific coast region and the prairies, there are fine anthologies to help students gain an understanding of the Maritimes, the provinces of the Atlantic coast. Literature focusing on the traditions, attitudes and way of life of the people who share this region are found in *Stories from Atlantic Canada,* edited by Kent Thompson, and *The Maritime Experience,* by Michael Nowlan. Literature linked with other regions of Canada such as the Far North, Southern Ontario and Quebec will be identified in discussions of the events and people of those regions. Other useful anthologies are *Stories from Western Canada,* by Rudy Wiebe, *Stories from Ontario,* by Germaine Warkentin, and *Stories from Quebec,* by Philip Stratford.

The First Canadians

Through historical accounts and literature Canada's native people — the Indian and the Eskimo or Inuit — have been portrayed in a variety of images ranging from that of cruel, violent savages quick to terrorize and slaughter white people to beings of noble, gracious bearing living in harmony with nature and easy victims of white people's racism and exploitation. Another overgeneralization is that native groups are all alike rather than being distinct cultural groups. Such a range of images is bound to have many students confused as to what the first Canadians were and actually are like.

One way to approach this topic is to follow the Siberian and Chinese ancestors of these native peoples as, during a period of 15,000 years, they spread east from Alaska across the vast wilderness of present-day Canada to the Atlantic coast and south to the furthest tip of South America. As the different tribes or clan groups settled in the highly varied areas — the sea coast, the mountains, the plains and the lakes and forests — their cultures became shaped more decisively by the environments they had chosen than by their heritage.

Perhaps the way of life of the six nations of the Pacific coast was the strongest and most distinctive. The rivers and sea ensured an abundant food supply; both land and sea made them rich in furs; and the tall cedars were the source of their houses, canoes and carvings. For grade 6-9 students, short, highly illustrated books such as *Eagle Mask* and *Ghost Paddle,* by James Houston, recreate the Northwest Coast Indian culture and provide details of daily life — salmon fishing; the whale hunt; styles of warfare; the importance of art, legend, song and dance; and the significance of the potlatch. Both books, accurate in details and illustrations, reflect the author's profound respect for the meaningfulness of Indian life, lore and art. For senior students Roderick Haig-Brown's *The Whale People* also describes Indian life before the coming of white people as it traces the training and maturation of a chief's son while he prepares to become chief of his tribe and a harpooner on a whaling canoe. This novel richly depicts the Haida culture and dramatizes the complexities of Indian economic and political patterns. For younger students *Nkwala,* by Edith Sharp, is also an anthropological novel, which describes the social setting and beliefs of the Spokan tribe in what is now British Columbia.

A picture of the consequences of an Indian tribe coming in contact with the white man is found in Christie Harris' *Raven's Cry.* In this novel she relates, from the Haida Indian point of view, white people's cruelty, foolishness and indifference toward Indians. Through their study of the Haida culture, students will also become more sensitive to the internal forces that contributed to the destruction of this powerful, sophisticated Indian nation.

Two novels for students in grades 6-9, *River of Stars,* by Jean Mackenzie, and *I Heard the Owl Call My Name,* by Margaret Craven, dramatically depict longer-range consequences of contact with white people. The former portrays a teenage boy

Totem Pole carved by the Haida Indians of Northwestern Canada

caught in a conflict between the Indian and white cultures, and the latter sensitively shows an Indian culture dying. Both novels provide opportunities to understand the role in British Columbia of Indian fishing rights, the reserve system and residential schools. Two novels for grade 10-12 students that also explore the consequences of contact between Indians and whites are *Mist on the River*, by Hubert Evans, and *Run Indian Run*, by Thomas Kelly. A realistic novel set in British Columbia in the 1950s, *Mist on the River* examines the choices open to a young adult Indian in conflict with white and Indian cultures. *Run Indian Run*, set in the early 1900s, is a powerful and exciting story of the circumstances surrounding two Indians who, although innocent of the murders of two white men, flee to the forests of British Columbia.

By shifting from a study of the coastal Indians to looking at the tribes of the prairies, teachers can highlight the unique characteristics of each. *The White Calf*, by Cliff Faulknor, and *The Wolfers*, by Lilian Pfeiffer, are novels that will help both junior and senior students gain an understanding of another Canadian-Indian culture. When the Plains Indians, dependent upon the buffalo for food and skins, acquired horses and later repeating rifles, they became superbly accomplished riders and marksmen. Military societies developed and a chief riding at full gallop with an eagle-feather headdress and banners and ribbons streaming from his lance or rifle and horse might remind the reader of a medieval knight.

Set in the 1850s, *The White Calf* dramatizes the daily routines of the Plains Indian life before large scale confrontation with white people. The setting of *The Wolfers* is the Great Plains, now southwestern Alberta, in the early 1870s after Rupert's Land had been acquired by Canada, but before any system of law had been estab-

lished. The "wolfers" were the free traders who, by smuggling whiskey into Canada for trading with the Indians, contributed to the destruction of their way of life. The strength of the novel lies in rich details of the lives of the Plains Indians as the readers see their camps, their councils, their initiation rites and dances, all of which were soon to disappear.

Other novels, particularly effective with grade 6-9 students, valuable for their portrayals of specific Indian tribes are *Agouhanna*, by Claude Aubry, and *No Word for Good-bye*, by John Craig. In *Agouhanna* the author successfully combines the history, tribal customs and folklore of the Iroquoian people. Set on Lake Kinniwaki near the Manitoba border, *No Word for Good-bye* demonstrates the difficulties the Ojibway people have encountered in their almost futile attempts to maintain their traditional way of life. For use with both junior and senior students, *I Am An Indian*, edited by Kent Gooderham, is a rich anthology of historical essays, journals, reminiscences, poems and songs by members of many of the Indian tribes of Canada. For students in grades 8-12, *Indian Legends of Canada*, by Claude Melancon, contains legends from the Pacific coast, the Prairies, the Eastern Woodlands and the Atlantic coast. Some of the distinctive traits of each of the four regions are described, and the legends themselves offer different Indian perceptions of the world.

There are several authors who write from a wide experience of the Arctic and a personal knowledge of the Eskimo or Inuit people. The most outstanding and prolific of these is James Houston. His knowledge of the Arctic is so deep rooted that details of culture and place are an integral part of his writing and art as he provides a glimpse of this formidable, mysterious world. Although basically stories of the struggle to survive in a land of constant peril and unbelievable hardship, the human concern and affection that characterize these northern people are ever present. Always they show gratitude and respect for animals, never killing more than necessary, wasting nothing as every part is utilized for food, clothing, fuel, utensils and weapons. Houston's drawings, many suggestive of Eskimo sculptures, authentically depict the unique aspects of the art and culture of the Inuit people.

For students in grades 6-9, *Tikta'Liktak*, *The White Archer*, *Akavak*, *Wolf Run* and *Long Claws* are all stories describing the traditional ways and wisdom of the Eskimos. On the other hand, *Frozen Fire* and *Black Diamonds* introduce inventions and concerns of the modern world — airplanes, helicopters, snowmobiles, oil rigs and drilling for oil. Although he has not filled his books for younger readers with his pessimism regarding white social impact upon this northern culture, Houston makes it clear that it is the Eskimo's knowledge of the old ways rather than a reliance upon modern technology that will continue to equip them to meet the challenges of their formidable environment.

Other books suitable for younger students are *Harpoon of the Hunter*, by Markoosie, *Pitseolak: Pictures Out of My Life*, by Pitseolak, and *Sons of the Arctic*, by Doug Wilkinson. Markoosie and Pitseolak are both Eskimo writers who, through their simple style and illustrations, effectively share the dangers associated with hunting polar bears as well as the traditional activities and ceremonies of daily life, work and play. Wilkinson's novel is also a traditional survival story, but contains details of modern Eskimo life, which are the result of the ever-increasing contact with modern white technology.

For students in grades 10-12, James Houston's novels *The White Dawn* and *Spirit Wrestler* dramatize the role of the shaman and the conflicts that result when a native culture is jolted by the arrival of outsiders. Based upon actual events, *The White Dawn* shows how three white men who came to live with them destroyed the Inuit's traditional ways of life. Set in Labrador, *White Eskimo*, by Harold Horwood, is the story of a "great white hunter" who wins the admiration of the Inuit and helps them overcome the effects of colonialism. This novel and *The White Dawn* would enrich a discussion of the Inuit as victims of foreign intrusion and exploitation. *The White Shaman*, by C. W. Nicol, is another novel that describes the challenge of the Arctic wilderness and the mystery of shamanism, a mixture of religion, medicine, magic and witchcraft.

Also for senior students are *People of the Deer* and *The Desperate People*, by Farley Mowat. The author lived for two years with the 49 survivors of the Ihalmiut tribe, a tribe of inland Eskimos of the Northwest Territories that once numbered in the thousands. Another fine collection of stories describing the challenge of this part of the world is Mowat's *The Snow Walker*.

An anthology of stories appropriate for both junior and senior students is *Stories from Pacific and Arctic Canada*, edited by Andreas Schroeder and Rudy Wiebe. Tales like "Walrus Hunt," "The Battle of the Drums," "Wolf Tracks" and "Men Like Summer Snow" are particularly valuable for understanding the culture of the Inuit people. Also worthwhile is *Native Peoples in Canadian Literature*, by William and Christine Mowat, a collection of speeches, poetry, stories and legends of both the Indian and Inuit peoples. Thematic questions to aid discussion and increase understanding of native cultures are also included.

An event that ties with the literature depicting Canada's north country and first peoples is the Yukon Gold Rush. *The Golden Trail: The Story of the Klondike Gold Rush*, by Pierre Berton, is based upon firsthand accounts, interviews by the author, diaries and published reports describing the Klondike between 1896 and 1899. Older students will also enjoy *I Married the Klondike*, by Laura Berton, Pierre Berton's mother who accepted a teaching position in Dawson City. She captures the mood of the time and of the decline following the great gold rush. Students in grades 6-9 will find *Gold-Fever Trail: A Klondike Adventure*, by Monica Hughes, exciting. Stories of the Cariboo Gold Rush in British Columbia will also increase students' understanding of the powerful lure of gold and its role in Canada's history. Particularly appropriate for younger readers are *Cariboo Runaway*, by Frances Duncan, *Cariboo Trail*, by Christie Harris, and *Quest in the Cariboo*, by John Hayes.

EXPLORERS AND EXPLORATION

Nowhere are the challenge of the wilderness landscape and bitter climate more apparent than in the biographies, historical accounts and novels portraying the early explorers. Containing short selections of interest to both junior and senior students is *The Top of the World Trilogy*, by Farley Mowat, which provides a rich variety of edited and annotated versions of the journals of explorers. *Ordeal by Ice* chronicles the search for the Northwest Passage; *The Polar Passion* describes the race to be first to the North Pole; and *Tundra* deals with the exploration of northern Canada.

For students in grades 6-9, two exciting descriptions of the search for the Northwest Passage are *Franklin of the Arctic* and *Mutiny in the Bay: Henry Hudson's Last Voyage*, by Richard Lambert. The former is a biography of the major happenings in Franklin's life, including his explorations and tragic death in the Arctic. The shocking and dramatic events of Hudson's last voyage make exciting reading because they

are based upon the journal of an eyewitness, Abacuk Pricket. Valuable for its writing and useful for comparing with Lambert's factual account is *Mutiny on Hudson Bay: A Story about the Last Voyage of Henry Hudson*, by Delbert Young. Young also blends history and fiction effectively in his novel *Last Voyage of the Unicorn*, an account of the ill-fated Munck expedition of 1619 searching for the Northwest Passage. In both novels Young uses the ship's cabin boy as the narrator.

Many well-written, accurate histories and biographies of the early explorers would be meaningful to junior students and of interest to those in grades 10-12. The following is a sampling, chosen primarily for the effective writing rather than the topic: *The Savage River: Seventy-One Days with Simon Fraser*, by Marjorie Campbell; *Alexander Mackenzie and the North West*, by Roy Daniells; *The True North: The Story of Captain Joseph Bernier* (the man who assured Canada's sovereignty over the Arctic), by Thomas Fairley and Charles Israel; *Captain of the Discovery: The Story of Captain George Vancouver*, by Roderick Haig-Brown; *North for Adventure*, the story of Samuel Hearne's overland trip to the Arctic, by Richard Lambert; *The First Canadian: The Story of Champlain*, by Cicero Ritchie; *David Thompson: Fur Trader, Explorer, Geographer*, by James Smith; and *The St. Lawrence*, by William Toye, an excellent collection of anecdotes, documents and maps.

EARLY SETTLEMENT

An introduction to the coming of the French to North America will help students understand why Canada today is a bilingual country. Anxious to compete with other European powers, France had a dream of extending its influence to the New World, then thought to be Asia. Beginning in 1534, Jacques Cartier made three exploratory expeditions to the Gulf of St. Lawrence and up the St. Lawrence River for the purpose of establishing settlements. However, partly because of religious wars in France, not until Samuel de Champlain's expeditions in 1608 was the first permanent French settlement, Quebec, established.

As the result of rewards to parents who raised large families and a program of sending young, unmarried women — "king's daughters," — to New France, the colony's population increased rapidly. *The King's Daughter*, by Suzanne Martel, is a beautifully written novel that describes the experiences of an eighteen-year-old orphan who is sent to Quebec to be the bride of an unknown settler. This novel, rich in its depiction of this period in history, will be enjoyed by both junior and senior students.

For the next 90 years the French explorers continued to claim lands and build forts for France as far south as the mouth of the Mississippi, north to Hudson Bay and west of Lake Superior. However, in 1670, in the name of the newly established Hudson's Bay Company, England claimed all the lands that drained into the great northern bay. As a result the English and the French were in constant conflict for control of the continent. Unlike the French colonists, who in the main were sent by France and were very dependent upon their mother country, the vast majority of the English settlers had chosen to come to America. The English population of the Thirteen Colonies grew to be almost 15 times the size of New France. Battle after battle saw France lose more and more territory to the English until in the Treaty of Paris in 1763, the French signed away their rights to Canada and 60,000 French Canadians came under British rule.

A number of novels and historical accounts dramatize specific aspects of the period outlined above. Two novels of particular interest to students in grades 10-12 are *The Golden Dog: A Romance of Old Quebec*, by William Kirby, and *The White and the Gold*, by Thomas Costain. Kirby's story, based upon fact, covers the period from 1748 to the fall of French Canada in 1763. *The White and the Gold* is a fuller account of the French regime in Canada and, although not always historically accurate, it is valuable for its vivid and interesting portrayal of people and events.

The following literary accounts are particularly suitable for students in grades 6-9. *Battle for the Rock: The Story of Wolfe and Montcalm*, by Joseph Schull, is an exciting reconstruction of the events leading up to the Battle of the Plains of Abraham and of the battle itself. *Fur Trader: The Story of Alexander Henry*, by Robert Ferguson, dramatically reveals how the British victory on the Plains of Abraham affected the Indians and the fur trade. *Adventurers from the Bay: Men of the Hudson's Bay Company*, by Clifford Wilson, is the history of the Company told through the exploits of some of its greatest traders such as Radisson, Kelsey and Hearne.

Introducing the competition to the Hudson's Bay Company is *The Nor'Westers: The Fight for the Fur Trade*, by Marjorie Campbell, a history of the North West Company and its struggle for supremacy in the fur trade. Insights into what life was like in a trading post are found in *The Reluctant Pioneer*, by Pearl Packard. The authentic facts are based upon the experiences of the author's grandmother, who was the wife of a Hudson's Bay factor posted 900 miles north of Lachine. Another book dealing with the Selkirk settlers is *Red River Adventure: The Story of the Selkirk Settlers*, by John Chalmers. Caught between the rivalries of the Hudson's Bay and the North West Companies, these early settlers struggle for existence in the early 1800s.

WARS AND REBELLIONS

A wealth of U.S. literature describing the people and events of the American War of Independence is available. Canadian historical fiction like the following that portrays the Loyalists, the Americans who supported the British during the revolution, will help students view the events from another perspective. The Loyalists, branded by many as traitors, were harshly treated, and persecuted; many were severely beaten or murdered. Between 1776 and 1783 over 40,000 Loyalists fled north into territory that remained British. After 1783 thousands more followed, most settling in Nova Scotia, but all found a land poorly prepared to accommodate such an increase in population. *Honor Bound,* by Mary Alice and John Downie, describes the flight of a Loyalist family from Philadelphia to political safety in Canada. This is excellent historical fiction that makes the reader vividly aware of the hardships endured by the family and of the incredible difficulties faced in settling in an undeveloped land. *Escape: Adventures of a Loyalist Family,* by Mary Fryer, is another well-written account based upon the experiences of that author's own family as they journeyed from Schenectady, New York, to Johnstown, Ontario. The constant fear of detection and arrest is effectively woven into a detailed description of the life of the period and of the hardships endured by the family. *On Loyalist Trails,* by John Hayes, is a third novel on this topic. All three are particularly appropriate for younger students, but would also be of interest to students in grades 10-12. A short, valuable essay summarizing this period is "An Influx of English: The King's 'Traitors'" in *Canadian Viewpoints: An Anthology of Canadian Writing.*

"Conflagration: The War of 1812," by Robert Collins in *Canadian Viewpoints,* is an excellent introduction to this rarely discussed war with its debatable outcome for the U.S. Two biographies that would enrich discussion of this topic by junior and senior students are *Tecumseh: The Story of the Shawnee Chief,* by Luella Creighton, and *The Good Soldier: The Story of Isaac Brock,* by Donald Goodspeed.

The personalities and events linked with the Upper Canada Rebellion of 1837 are described in a number of histories and biographies suitable for students in grades 6-9. A key figure in this rebellion was William Lyon Mackenzie, subject of a biography by David Flint titled *William Lyon Mackenzie: Rebel Against Authority.* The events are presented with clarity, interest and fairness towards the protagonists on both sides. *The Boy With an R in His Hand,* by James Reaney, quickly introduces the social conditions and the conflicts between the Tories and the Grits that led to the Rebellion ten years later. The young protagonist, an apprentice in the newspaper office of William Lyon Mackenzie, witnesses the destruction of the printing press by a group of young Tories. The colorful characters, events and details give the reader a vivid picture of "muddy York" during the years prior to the Rebellion. Two other novels focusing on this event are *Rebel on the Trail,* by Lyn Cook, and *Rebels Ride at Night,* by John Hayes. An editorial written by Mackenzie ten days before the march on York entitled "To the Farmers of York County" is in the *Oxford Anthology of Canadian Literature,* edited by Robert Weaver and William Toye.

No one in Canadian history has aroused more passions and bitterness than the Métis chieftain Louis Riel. At first associated with the traditional rivalries of French Catholic Quebec and English Protestant Ontario, the basic conflict, as history has allowed us to see it, was the clash between primitive and civilized peoples. The two rebellions associated with Riel's name were the last organized attempts by Canada's primitive peoples to preserve their culture and identity. The failure of these rebellions and the execution of Louis Riel assured the domination of white cultures. Students in grades 6-9 will enjoy Hartwell Bowsfield's biography *Louis Riel: The Rebel and the Hero* and *Revolt in the West: The Story of the Riel Rebellion*, by Edward McCourt. Also of interest is *A Very Small Rebellion*, by Jan Truss, a fiction effectively interspersed with non-fiction chapters to provide a history of the Riel rebellion.

Of value to senior students are "Louis Riel and the Prairie Uprisings," by George F. G. Stanley in *Canadian Viewpoints*, and *Strange Empire: Louis Riel and the Métis People*, by Joseph Howard. Two plays suitable for in-class reading and discussion with students in grades 10-12 are *The Trial of Louis Riel*, by John Coulter, and *Tales from a Prairie Drifter*, by Rod Langley. Coulter's play is a re-enactment of the courtroom drama that resulted in Riel's execution for his part in the Métis uprising of 1885. The play by Langley brings together the Métis, the railway and the government in order to demonstrate some of the connections between various historical events in the West. Resources of value to both junior and senior students are the previously mentioned *I Am An Indian*, by Kent Gooderham, and *The Life of Louis Riel*, by Peter Charlebois, a book useful for its fine collection of archival pictures.

CANADA SINCE CONFEDERATION

Brief, well-written descriptions of the events surrounding the signing of the British North America Act in 1867 and of John A. MacDonald, the first prime minister of the new Dominion of Canada, are found in the highly recommended and previously mentioned *Canadian View-points*, edited by Allen Andrews, Diane Thompson and Douglas Cronk. This excellent collection includes short essays that highlight the impact of specific world events upon Canada: "The Great War," "The Thirties: A Crash Course in the Facts of Life" and "The Second World War." Allen Andrews also provides a valuable review of the major events of post war Canada in his essay "The Shaping of Modern Canada: 1945-1981."

One of the major events described by Andrews is known as the October or FLQ crisis of 1970, an event he believes "forced the rather self-satisfied Canadian populace into the realities of the new decade." For students in grades 10-12, Hugh MacLennan's novel *Return of the Sphinx* provides insight into the situation in Quebec in the 1960s by dramatizing the opposing points of view of the French-Canadian and English-Canadian cultures. His earlier novel, *Two Solitudes*, also helps to explain the reasons for the differences between the two peoples. Dealing with the actual October crisis, an interesting and exciting book for all high school students is *The Revolution Script*, by Brian Moore. Although factual, the book is written as if it were a novel with the author attempting to convey the thoughts and motivations of the different people and factions involved.

A novel to help deepen younger students' understanding of the impact and consequences of the Depression is *Billy Higgins Rides the Freights*, by Gloria Montero, the story of a family's struggle to combat the effects of the Depression. Thirteen-year-old Billy leaves school to find employment, becomes involved in the political activities of the unemployed in Vancouver, and joins thousands of "trekkers" riding the freights to Ottawa to demand jobs. More appropriate for older students is *Cabbagetown* by Hugh Garner, a very complete picture of the effect of the social, economic and political conditions of the Depression. Two valuable collections that will increase students' understanding of the atmosphere and the events of the 1930s are *Ten Lost Years*, by Barry Broadbent, and *The Winter Years*, by James Gray. Broadbent has compiled dozens of reminiscences of people from every province who struggled to survive during that bleak period in history. In *The Winter Years*, a collection of personal anecdotes, reflections and factual material, Gray provides many details of the social and economic situation during the Depression.

MULTICULTURAL SOCIETY

Awareness of the number of ethnic groups comprising Canada's population is provided by the literature linked with early exploration and settlement, the land, the first Canadians, and the relationships between the English and the French. Other fine literature is available to further increase students' consciousness of the rich cultural diversity characterizing Canada.

Although the influx of peoples around the turn of this century was larger than at any other time, immigration is a continuing process, the concerns of the first generation becoming those of subsequent generations. Always there is a fluctuating between the desire to integrate and the desire to retain one's cultural identity. Two basic conflicts dramatized in the related literature, particularly that for older students, are between parents and their children and between charter groups and the newly arrived. It is interesting to note that the two major adolescent crises — conflict with parents and search for identity — are also those experienced by the immigrant regardless of era. Two short stories that capture these complex feelings and the early experiences of the immigrant are Frederick Philip Grove's "The First Day of an Immigrant," in *Stories from Western Canada*, edited by Rudy Wiebe,

and Gabrielle Roy's "The Well of Dunrea," in *The Immigrant Experience*, edited by Leuba Bailey. Also valuable for work with high school students is the discussion of immigration found in the introduction of the collection by Bailey.

Many excellent books portraying specific ethnic groups now in Canada have been written for the younger reader. *Underground to Canada*, by Barbara Smucker, describes the daring escape of two young black girls from a southern cotton plantation where they were slaves. This exciting novel provides a historically accurate and detailed picture of the "underground railway" from Mississippi to St. Catherines, Ontario. Two other cultural groups and their emigration to Canada and life there are subjects of two fine novels also by Smucker, *Amish Adventure* and *Days of Terror*. The former is the story of the Amish who sought religious freedom, first in Pennsylvania and later in Southern Ontario. *Days of Terror* tells of a Mennonite family who joined the mass migration from Russia to Canada when the events of the Russian Revolution threatened the lives of these prosperous, nonviolent people living in the Ukraine. An introduction to this culture for older students is *Peace Shall Destroy Many*, by Rudy Wiebe. Also dramatizing the Mennonite's faith in nonviolence, this novel is set on a Mennonite farming settlement in Saskatchewan during World War II.

The perspective of some people of the oriental cultures living in Canada are found in literature particularly appropriate for middle and junior high school students. In *West Coast China Boy*, Lim Sing records, with colorful sketches, his memories of his boyhood in Vancouver's Chinatown around World War I. Effectively making readers aware of a shameful episode in Canadian history, *A Child in Prison Camp*, by Shizuye Takashima, is the author's account of life in a Canadian prison camp during World War II. She and her family were among the 22,000 people of Japanese origin stripped of their civil rights and property and, "for security reasons," removed from the coast of British Columbia for the duration of the war. Dramatizing the universality of racism, *Kap-Sung Ferris*, by Frances Duncan, tells of a young Korean girl who, after being falsely accused of shoplifting, is forced to come to terms with her Korean heritage.

Literature of the kind introduced in this chapter offers social studies teachers an opportunity to make the places, events and people of Canada more meaningful and memorable to a wide range of students.

Bibliography

Andrews, Allen, Diane Thompson, and Douglas Cronk, eds. *Canadian Viewpoints: An Anthology of Canadian Writing*. Victoria: Ministry of Education, Province of British Columbia, 1983.

Atwood, Margaret. *Survival: A Thematic Guide to Canadian Literature*. Toronto: Anansi, 1972.

Aubry, Claude. *Agouhanna*. Translated from the French by Harvey Swados. Illustrated by Julie Brinckloc. Toronto: Doubleday, 1972.

Bailey, Leuba, ed. *The Immigrant Experience*. Toronto: Macmillan, 1975.

Berton, Laura Beatrice. *I Married the Klondike*. Toronto: McClelland and Stewart, 1972.

Berton, Pierre. *The Golden Trail: The Story of the Klondike Gold Rush*. Illustrated by Duncan Macpherson. Toronto: Macmillan, 1954.

Bowsfield, Hartwell. *Louis Riel: The Rebel and the Hero*. Toronto: Oxford University Press, 1971.

Broadbent, Barry. *Ten Lost Years*. Toronto: Doubleday, 1973.

Campbell, Marjorie. *The Savage River: Seventy-One Days With Simon Fraser*. Toronto: Macmillan, 1968.

Chalmers, John. *Red River Adventure: The Story of the Selkirk Settlers*. Illustrated by Lewis Parker. Toronto: Macmillan, 1956.

Charlebois, Peter. *The Life of Louis Riel*. Toronto: NC Press, 1975.

Cook, Lyn. *Rebel on the Trail*. Toronto: Macmillan, 1953.

Costain, Thomas. *The White and the Gold*. Toronto: Doubleday, 1970.

Coulter, John. *The Trial of Louis Riel*. Ottawa: Oberon Press, 1969.

Craig, John. *No Word for Good-bye*. Toronto: Peter Martin Associates, 1969.

Craven, Margaret. *I Heard the Owl Call My Name*. Don Mills, Ontario: Collins, 1975; New York: Doubleday 1973, and Dell paperback, 1974.

Creighton, Luella. *Tecumseh: A Story of the Shawnee Chief*. Illustrated by William Lytle. Toronto: Macmillan, 1965.

Daniells, Roy. *Alexander Mackenzie and the North West*. Toronto: Oxford University Press, 1971.

Dawe, Alan, ed. *Roughing It in the Bush*. Toronto: McClelland and Stewart New Canadian Library, 1962.

Downie, Mary Alice, and John Downie. *Honor Bound*. Illustrated by Joan Huffman. Toronto: Oxford University Press, 1971.

Duncan, Frances. *Cariboo Runaway*. Illustrated by Karen Munteau. Toronto: Burns and MacEachern, 1976.

Duncan, Frances. *Kap-Sung Ferris*. Toronto: MacMillan, 1977.

Egoff, Sheila. *The Republic of Childhood: A Critical Guide to Canadian Children's Literature in English*, 2nd ed., Toronto: Oxford University Press, 1975.

Evans, Hubert. *Mist on the River*. Toronto: M and S New Canadian Library, 1973.

Fairley, Thomas C., and Charles E. Israel. *The True North: The Story of Captain Joseph Bernier*. Illustrated by James Hill. Toronto: Macmillan, 1957.

Faulkner, Cliff. *The White Calf*. Illustrated by Gerald Tailfeathers. Toronto: Little, Brown & Co., 1965.

Ferguson, Robert. *Fur Trader: The Story of Alexander Henry*. Illustrated by Douglas Sneyd. Toronto: Macmillan, 1961.

Flint, David. *William Lyon Mackenzie: Rebel Against Authority*. Toronto: Oxford University Press, 1971.

Frye, Northrup. *The Bush Garden: Essays on The Canadian Imagination*. Toronto: Anansi, 1972.

Fryer, Mary. *Escape: Adventures of a Loyalist Family*. Don Mills, Ontario: J. M. Dent & Sons, 1976.

Garner, Hugh. *Cabbagetown*. Markham, Ont.: Simon and Schuster, 1971.

Geddes, Gary, ed. *Skookum Wawa: An Anthology of the Canadian Northwest*. Toronto: Oxford University Press, 1975.

Gooderham, Kent, ed. *I Am An Indian*. Toronto: J. M. Dent and Sons, 1969.

Goodspeed, Donald. *The Good Soldier: The Story of Isaac Brock*. Illustrated by Jack Ferguson. Toronto: Macmillan, 1964.

Gray, James H. *The Winter Years*. Toronto: Macmillan, 1973.

Haig-Brown, Roderick. *Captain of the Discovery: The Story of Captain George Vancouver*. Illustrated by Robert Banks. Toronto: Macmillan, 1956.

Haig-Brown, Roderick. *Saltwater Summer*. New York: Morrow, 1948.

Haig-Brown, Roderick. *Starbuck Valley Winter*. New York: Morrow, 1943.

Haig-Brown, Roderick. *The Whale People*. Illustrated by Mary Weiler. Don Mills, Ont.: Collins, 1962.

Harris, Christie. *Cariboo Trail*. Toronto: Longman, 1957.

Harris, Christie. *Raven's Cry*. Illustrations by Bill Reid. Toronto/Montreal: McClelland and Stewart, 1966.

Hayes, John F. *On Loyalist Trails*. Illustrated by J. Merle Smith. Toronto: Copp Clark, 1971.

Hayes, John F. *Quest in the Cariboo*. Illustrated by Fred J. Finley. Toronto: Copp Clark, 1960.

Hayes, John F. *Rebels Ride at Night*. Illustrated by Fred J. Finley. Toronto: Copp Clark, 1953.

Henry, Alexander. *Travels and Adventures in Canada and the Indian Territories between the Years 1760 and 1776*. Edmonton: Hurtig, 1969.

Horwood, Harold. *White Eskimo*. Markham, Ont.: PaperJacks, 1973.

Houston, James. *Adavak: An Eskimo Journey*. New York: Harcourt, Brace & World; Toronto: Longman, 1968.

Houston, James. *Black Diamonds: Secrets of an Arctic Island*. New York: Atheneum; Toronto/Montreal: McClelland and Stewart, 1982.

Houston, James. *Eagle Mask: A West Coast Indian Tale*. New York: Harcourt, Brace & World; Toronto: Longman, 1966.

Houston, James. *Frozen Fire: A Tale of Courage*. New York: Atheneum; Toronto: McClelland and Stewart 1977.

Houston, James. *Ghost Paddle: A Northwest Coast Indian Tale*. New York: Harcourt Brace Jovanovich; Toronto: Longman, 1972.

Houston, James. *Long Claws: An Arctic Adventure*. New York: Atheneum; Toronto: McClelland and Stewart, 1981.

Houston, James. *Spirit Wrestler*. New York: Harcourt Brace Jovanovich; Toronto: McClelland and Stewart, 1980.

Houston, James. *Tikta'Liktak: An Eskimo Legend*. New York: Harcourt Brace & World; Toronto: Longman, 1965.

Houston, James. *The White Archer: An Eskimo Legend*. New York: Harcourt Brace & World; Toronto: Longman, 1971.

Houston, James. *The White Dawn*. New York: Harcourt Brace Jovanovich; Toronto: Longman, 1971.

Houston, James. *Wolf Run: A Caribou Eskimo Tale*. New York: Harcourt Brace Jovanovich, 1971.

Howard, Joseph. *Strange Empire: Louis Riel and the Métis People*. Toronto: James Lorimer, 1974.

Hughes, Monica. *Gold-Fever Trail: A Klondike Adventure*. Edmonton: LeBel Enterprises, 1974.

Kelly, Thomas. *Run Indian Run*. Markham, Ont.: PaperJacks, 1972.

Kirby, William. *The Golden Dog: A Romance of Old Quebec*. Toronto: McClelland and Stewart New Canadian Library, 1969.

Kurelek, William. *A Prairie Boy's Summer*. Montreal: Tundra, 1975.

Kurelek, William. *A Prairie Boy's Winter*. Paintings by the author. Montreal: Tundra, 1973.

Lambert, Richard. *Franklin of the Arctic*. Maps by Julius Griffith. Toronto: McClelland and Stewart, 1949.

Lambert, Richard. *Mutiny in the Bay: Henry Hudson's Last Voyage*. Illustrated by Joe Rosenthal. Toronto: Macmillan, 1963.

Lambert, Richard. *North for Adventure*. Illustrated by Vernon Mould. Toronto: McClelland and Stewart, 1952.

Langley, Rod. *Tales from a Prairie Drifter*. Toronto: Playwrights Co-op, 1974.

Littlejohn, Bruce, and Jon Pearce, eds. *Marked by the Wild: An Anthology of Canadian Literature Shaped by the Canadian Wilderness*. Toronto: McClelland and Stewart, 1973.

Mackenzie, Jean. *River of Stars*. Toronto: McClelland and Stewart, 1971.

MacLennan, Hugh. *The Return of the Sphinx*. Toronto: Macmillan, 1967.

MacLennan, Hugh. *Two Solitudes*. Toronto: Macmillan, 1968.

Markoosie. *Harpoon of the Hunter.* Illustrations by Germaine Arnaktauyok. Montreal/London: McGill-Queen's, 1970.

Martel, Suzanne. *The King's Daughter.* Vancouver: Douglas and McIntyre, 1980.

McCourt, Edward. *Revolt in the West: The Story of the Riel Rebellion.* Illustrated by Jack Ferguson. Toronto: Macmillan, 1958 (Great Stories of Canada).

Melancon, Claude. *Indian Legends of Canada.* Agincourt, Ont.: Gage Educational Publishing, 1974.

Mitchell, W. O. *Who Has Seen the Wind.* Toronto: Macmillan, 1961.

Montero, Gloria. *Billy Higgins Rides the Freights.* Toronto: James Lorimer, 1982.

Moodie, Susanna. *Roughing It in the Bush.* Toronto: McClelland and Stewart New Canadian Library, 1962.

Moore, Brian. *The Revolution Script.* Markham, Ont.: Simon and Schuster, 1972.

Moss, John. *Patterns of Isolation.* Toronto: McClelland and Stewart, 1974.

Mowat, Farley. *The Desperate People.* Toronto: McClelland and Stewart, 1975.

Mowat, Farley. *People of the Deer.* Toronto: McClelland and Stewart, 1975.

Mowat, Farley. *The Snow Walker.* Toronto: McClelland and Stewart, 1975.

Mowat, Farley. *The Top of the World Trilogy.* Toronto: McClelland and Stewart, 1973 (boxed set). *Ordeal by Ice* (1960), *The Polar Passion* (1967), *Tundra* (1973).

Mowat, William, and Christine Mowat, eds. *Native People in Canadian Literature.* Toronto: Macmillan, 1972.

Nicol, C. W. *The White Shaman.* Toronto: McClelland and Stewart, 1979.

Packard, Pearl. *The Reluctant Pioneer.* Montreal: Palm Publishers, 1968.

Pfeiffer, Lilian. *The Wolfers.* Illustrated by David Craig. Toronto: Burns and MacEachern, 1967.

Reaney, James. *The Boy With an R in His Hand.* Illustrated by Leo Rampen. Toronto: Macmillan, 1965.

Ritchie, Cicero. *The First Canadian: The Story of Champlain.* Illustrated by William Wheeler. Toronto: Macmillan, 1961.

Ross, Sinclair. *The Lamp at Noon and Other Stories.* McClelland and Stewart New Canadian Library, 1968.

Schroeder, Andreas, and Rudy Wiebe, eds. *Stories from Pacific and Arctic Canada.* Toronto: Macmillan, 1974.

Schull, Joseph. *Battle for the Rock: The Story of Wolfe and Montcalm.* Illustrated by Lewis Parker. Toronto: Macmillan, 1960.

Sharp, Edith. *Nkwala.* Illustrated by William Winter. Boston: Little, Brown & Co., 1958.

Sing, Lim. *West Coast Chinese Boy.* Montreal: Tundra, 1979.

Smith, James. *David Thompson: Fur Trader, Explorer, Geographer.* Toronto: Oxford University Press, 1971.

Smucker, Barbara. *Amish Adventure.* Toronto: Clarke, Irwin & Co., 1983.

Smucker, Barbara. *Days of Terror.* Toronto: Clarke, Irwin & Co., 1979.

Smucker, Barbara. *Underground to Canada.* Toronto: Clarke, Irwin & Co., 1977. (Published in the United States as *Runaway to Freedom.* New York: Harper & Row, 1978.)

Stratford, Philip, ed. *Stories from Quebec.* Toronto: Van Nostrand Reinhold, 1974.

Takashima, Shizuye. *A Child in Prison Camp.* Montreal: Tundra Books, 1971.

Thompson, Kent, ed. *Stories from Atlantic Canada.* Toronto: Macmillan, 1973.

Thompson, Michael, *The Maritime Experience.* Toronto: Macmillan, 1975.

Toye, William. *The St. Lawrence.* Illustrated by Leo Rampen. Toronto: Oxford University Press, 1959.

Truss, Jan. *A Very Small Rebellion.* With an essay by Jack Chambers. Edmonton: J. J. LeBel Enterprises Ltd., 1977.

Warkentin, Germaine, ed. *Stories from Ontario.* Toronto: Macmillan, 1974.

Weaver, Robert, and William Toye, eds. *Oxford Anthology of Canadian Literature.* Toronto: Oxford University Press, 1973.

Wiebe, Rudy, ed. *Stories from Western Canada.* Toronto: Macmillan, 1972.

Wiebe, Rudy. *Peace Shall Destroy Many.* Toronto: M & S New Canadian Library, 1964.

Wilkinson, Doug. *Sons of the Arctic.* Illustrated by Prudence Seward. Toronto: Clarke, Irwin, 1965.

Wilson, Clifford. *Adventurers from the Bay: Men of the Hudson's Bay Company.* Illustrated by Lloyd Scott. Toronto: Macmillan, 1962.

Young, Delbert. *Mutiny on Hudson Bay: A Story About the Last Voyage of Henry Hudson.* Illustrated by Doug Sneyd. Toronto: Gage, 1963.

Young, Delbert, *Last Voyage of the Unicorn.* Illustrated by Mary Cserepy. Toronto/Vancouver: Clarke, Irwin & Co., 1969.

Student Activities

Sutton provides the reader with a unique perspective on Canada revealed through its literature. Through the use of literary works, students can develop a fuller understanding of a place and its people. Literature, combined with descriptive and analytical social science information, can provide a powerful base for increasing student motivation and adding vitality to social studies. It is the goal of the author that the reader select at least one source from the wide array, locate it in the library, read it and be ready to share the key ideas with other members of the class.

According to Russell B. Nye,[1] an authority on Canadian authors, "In reading Canadian literature, it is important to remember that it is not 'American' literature, rather it is 'North American.' Like earlier American literature, Canadian writing had a hard time establishing its identity. Always facing the powerful pull toward England, France, and the United States, the Canadian writers' problem has been survival and the need for developing a sense of who they are."

The following activities are intended to help students use Canadian literature in learning about this nation.

1.   A Linear Chart: A Great Aid for Preparing Your Oral Report

Select one of the sources described in Sutton's article, then organize an oral report that responds to these questions:

What is the name of the book?
What is the theme?
Who are the main characters?
What were the most significant events?

[1]Russell B. Nye, "On Canadian Literature," in *A Canadian Vocabulary*, ed. Victor Howard (East Lansing, MI: 1981), 246.

After you have identified the key elements you wish to present, make a linear chart. To do this, draw a series of illustrations depicting significant aspects of the story and the report. Attach these illustrations (make sure they are large enough for the audience to see) to a piece of yarn with masking tape. These will serve as visual referents for your presentation. Linear charting can also assist you in sorting out the major ideas and the supporting ones.

Try this approach. It's helpful, it adds interest and your classmates will enjoy it!

2.   Dare You Compare?

Select one of the sources described in Sutton's article. Use the following as a guide for comparing the literary source to what you have learned in class about Canada or to the facts found in the text or other references.

A.   Find evidence that contradicts or challenges the "facts."
B.   Find evidence that confirms the facts.
C.   What new ideas did you derive as a result of reading the literary work?
D.   Are these supported or refuted in the text or other reference books? Give *specific* examples.
E.   What generalization can you make about the literary work that you read?
F.   Would you recommend it to a friend? Why or why not?

3.   Try Your Hand at an Art Project

After reading one of the literary works described by Sutton, create a papier-mâché model or diorama of the place described. Be ready to give a brief presentation about the book using your art form to enhance your effort.

4. So What Can You Learn From a Fictionalized Account?

Read one of the sources described by Sutton. As you reflect on it, ask yourself the following questions and document each response by citing specific examples:

A. Did the author embellish the facts by adding events, inventing conversation, introducing ideas that may not actually have occurred, oversimplifying events?

B. Are you able to participate vicariously in the historical period by seeing the sights, feeling the emotions, being a part of the events as they occurred?

C. What major issue provided the focus?

D. What did the author seem to value?

E. Was the author successful? Why? Why not?

F. Would you recommend this literary work to a friend? Why? Why not?

G. Would you like to be an author of fiction? Why? Why not?

Share your responses with a peer or write an editorial about the book you read. Use the questions and responses as a guide.

5. How Successful Are You as a Salesperson?

After reading one of the many books suggested by Sutton, prepare a brief sales pitch for your peers. Include at least one propaganda technique in your presentation. Suggested techniques include: name calling, glittering generality, transfer, testimonial, card stacking, plainfolks device, and bandwagon technique. Keep in mind that you need to have a "capturing" beginning and succinct closing. Ask each classmate to record a "YES, I'd buy the book" or "NO, I would not" based on your presentation. Ask each to give at least one reason for his or her response. (You are to assume the book is not available at any library and that you have sufficient funds to buy at least ten books for classmates.)

CHAPTER **6**

French Canada

RICHARD BEACH
AND
MARTIN LUBIN

The timing, location and pattern of early French exploration and colonization of North America varied from that of other Europeans who vied for control of the continent. Compared with most European countries, organized efforts by the French began earlier. Yet their exploration exhibited a rather narrow regional focus, since it was almost entirely in the northeast coastal area; interest and support of the French government waxed and waned; the economy was overwhelmingly mono-product oriented (fish, then fur) and dependent upon exports to the mother country; and religion played an important if not vital role in the colonial society as well as in the exploration effort itself.

Notwithstanding John Cabot's English-supported voyages along the coast of Newfoundland during the 1490s, the French sponsored the first serious attempts to explore and claim for France what is presently Canada. French fishing fleets first plied the coastline around the turn of the 16th century. The Italian Verrazano, under the French flag, explored and mapped sections of the eastern archipelago during the 1520s. Several years later French adventurer Jacques Cartier, with the support of

King Francis I, explored the coastline and became the first European to penetrate the heart of the continent in search of gold and a route to the Orient.

In 1534, during the first of his three voyages, Cartier explored the Gulf of St. Lawrence and established contact with the native peoples along the Gaspé Peninsula. He returned to France the same year full of enthusiasm and imaginative Indian tales of the exotic "Kingdom of the Saguenay" in the interior. The next year, he skirted the islands of Newfoundland, Cape Breton, Prince Edward and Anticosti, and again explored the Gulf of St. Lawrence. Most important, he traveled up the St. Lawrence River as far as the rapids near the Island of Montreal. The expedition, however, was fraught with disaster. Cartier and his fearless adventurers decided to winter near the Indian village of Stadacona (Quebec City). The men were ill-equipped to cope with the rigors of the "Canadian" environment and many died of starvation and disease. Cartier and the survivors returned to France the next spring with no concrete evidence of wealth or knowledge of the illusory kingdom.

Undaunted, he was successful six years

later in persuading the authorities to attempt another voyage. No route to the Orient was found, the native population was far less friendly, having been ill-treated and exploited by Cartier previously, and little wealth other than exotic flora and fauna was discovered. The failure of these expeditions coupled with important preoccupations in Europe resulted in the French government abandoning for nearly 75 years any further attempts at exploration or settlement in the New World. Whatever early advantage the French, in competition with their European rivals, could have had to establish a permanent foothold, and a claim to the continent, therefore, was lost.

During the French hiatus, explorers, traders and fishermen, as individuals or representatives of other European governments and commercial interests, explored the coastline of North America from Florida to Labrador. The novelty of their adventures stirred the imaginations (and bank accounts) of entrepreneurs, but little of value was found except an abundance of fish. Although individual Frenchmen probably continued fishing and trading with the Indians during the late 1500s, not until 1603 with the arrival of soldier-geographer and "Father of French Canada," Samuel de Champlain, did the French make a renewed effort to explore and to settle Canada. Thereafter, a French presence and influence in North America became firmly established.

Champlain and his partner de Monts attempted a settlement on an island in the St. Croix River, now the Maine-New Brunswick border. Although this first effort was a failure, two years later a far more suitable site was chosen in the Annapolis Valley in what is now the Province of Nova Scotia. Port Royal, as the little fortress was called, subsequently became the center of Acadia, France's first permanent colony in Canada.

Furs, especially beaver, had superseded fish as the motive of most commercial venture in northern North America.[1] Aware that this resource was far more plentiful in the interior, Champlain in 1608 retraced Cartier's steps up the St. Lawrence in search of a location for a French settlement nearer the heart of the beaver's domain. The site he chose lay below the cliffs of Quebec City. For several decades L'Abitation served as the center of the French commercial and political empire in North America.

The growth of the colonies in Acadia and along the St. Lawrence was extremely slow during the 17th and 18th centuries. The support of French authorities was for the most part half-hearted or indifferent. Geopolitical preoccupations in Europe and the attraction of greater wealth and resources elsewhere in the French colonial empire precluded much interest in expanding and subsequently consolidating and protecting the dispersed and underpopulated North American colonies. Few people were willing to emigrate from France to these fledgling colonies. Especially unattractive to potential settlers were the inhospitable climate and physical environment, the terror of Indian warfare and raids, and a quasi-feudal system of land tenure based on large tracts of land known as seigneuries.

Moreover, economic structures established by the French government did not encourage expansive settlement. The economy and land settlement policy of Nouvelle France remained inextricably linked to the fur trade and was, until at least the 1660s, rigidly monopolistic. Indeed, the fur trade by its very nature often precluded the establishment of a settled and orderly way of life in the colony. Ex-

---

[1]The fur trade, unlike the fishing industry — which did not stimulate much exploration or permanent settlement at first — inaugurated and indeed epitomized the cyclical pattern of natural resource exploration, which was to continue for nearly 400 years.

pansion of the fur trading web, without either parallel expansion of economic and political infrastructures or immigration from France, merely weakened the already tenuous hold that French military and religious leaders had upon the lives and lands under their jurisdiction.

Throughout the 17th century, however, the indomitable and legendary *coureurs de bois* — French explorers like LaVérendrye and de la Salle — and courageous Roman Catholic missionaries — like Joliet and Marquette — crisscrossed more than half the continent, exploring, mapping the land, and spreading Christianity among the native people. By the end of the 17th century, the French empire stretched in a huge arc from the Gulf of St. Lawrence, through the entire region of the Great Lakes to the Rockies, into the Ohio Valley, and down the Mississippi to the Gulf of Mexico. Except for the colonies in Acadia and along the St. Lawrence, however, where permanent settlements were rooted, only a scattered system of forts and fur trading posts existed to maintain French control over the millions of square miles of territory.

The French empire in North America had reached its apogee by the turn of the 18th century and signs of the inevitable collapse appeared soon after. As early as the 1670s, an encirclement began as the British established footholds in Hudson Bay to the north and along the coasts of Newfoundland and Nova Scotia to the east. Most significantly, the string of French outposts in the "West" presented a hindrance and a menace to the increasingly expansionist-minded English (American) colonies to the south.

Reflecting French military and diplomatic failures in Europe, rather than significant military defeats in the New World, the Treaty of Utrecht, signed by the French and the British in 1713, nevertheless signaled the disintegration of the French em-

pire in North America. The Hudson Bay region, Newfoundland and French Acadia were ceded to the British, leaving only Ile St. Jean (Prince Edward Island) and Ile Royale (Cape Breton Island), with the formidable fortress of Louisbourg, to guard the St. Lawrence colony. These changes effectively reduced the threat of French raids along the coast and protected the English fishing fleets. For the next 40 years, the struggle between the British and French intensified, with economic and political control of the North American continent the prize.

The final chapter in the long-festering conflict between the two European rivals was written in the 1750s. The odds against French success were overwhelming. The population of the English colonies by then was nearly 2 million, while the French numbered fewer than 80,000. Moreover, France had become increasingly involved in European wars and virtually left the people of Nouvelle France to fend for themselves. British probings along the east coast increased and the Iroquois, long the scourge of the French colonies, harassed the dispersed and undermanned French outposts.

Owing to British inexperience in the ways of wilderness warfare, the French initially repelled the attacks and even had some successes.[2] The British inevitably gained the upper hand.[3] With their superior fleet and arms, they captured Louisbourg in 1758, leaving the entire French colony along the St. Lawrence vulnerable to attack. The next year, General Wolfe defeated the French at Quebec City in one of the most important battles ever fought

---

[2]One of the early French victories took place at Fort Necessity in the Ohio Valley against a young British colonel, George Washington.

[3]One of the saddest chapters in Canadian history was written in 1755, when the British expelled the Acadians from their homeland in Nova Scotia and Ile St. Jean. Most of the population was dispersed throughout the English colonies to the south, an event vividly depicted in Longfellow's poem "Evangeline."

on the North American continent. Within months, Three Rivers and Montreal surrendered. The Treaty of Paris, signed in 1763, ceded the entire French empire in Canada to the British, except for two small islands in the Gulf of St. Lawrence. Most of the French nobility and some of the bourgeoisie returned to France, leaving 60,000 peasants, *les habitants,* and some lower echelon clergy to fend for themselves under British rule.

French Canada in the latter half of the 18th century was comprised of the little colony along the St. Lawrence and pockets of Acadians located throughout what were to become the Maritime Provinces. Surprisingly, these conservative, Catholic, land-based French-speaking people survived, even flourished, under the control of their aggressive, entrepreneurial, Protestant, and English-speaking masters.

Several events ensured their survival. In 1774 the British government passed the Quebec Act, giving the French the right to their language, religion and certain civil laws. This major concession to the population of "Quebec" was a de jure, but not yet de facto, acceptance and recognition of a French-speaking province within the British Empire. There was, of course, a very pragmatic and strategic rationale for the passage of this Act — to placate the French and at least neutralize them should revolt occur in the refractory "American" colonies to the south. Despite the apparently magnanimous tenor of the Quebec Act, the British fully expected that with an infusion of British settlers and, after 1780, "Loyalist" refugees and immigrants from the United States, the French-speaking population would eventually be assimilated. They were wrong. Isolated from the mother country, and economically and culturally alienated from the British and Americans, but with the guarantee of their fundamental rights, the French Canadian population during the last decades of the

18th century turned inward, remaining almost oblivious to the English political and commercial environment around them. They depended more heavily than ever upon the church for leadership and inspiration. Especially in the Quebec colony, the lusty indigenous population grew rapidly as a result of an extraordinarily high birthrate and relatively low death rate. By the turn of the century, the survival of the French-speaking population was virtually assured; some segments of the bourgeoisie and clerical elites even sought accommodation with the English leaders.

Yet the British were never comfortable with this rapidly expanding, though basically passive, population in their midst. Several ill-founded and unsuccessful efforts were made to assimilate or at least to suppress French attempts to obtain political influence. The Constitutional Act of 1791, for example, subdivided the large Quebec colony into two parts — Upper Canada, the territory surrounding the Great Lakes (which subsequently became the Province of Ontario), and Lower Canada (the seigneurial land straddling the St. Lawrence and Richlieu Rivers (later to become the Province of Quebec). The minority English population in the old Quebec colony, most of whom had settled west of Montreal, thus avoided potential domination by the more numerous French Canadians living in the St. Lawrence Lowland. The Act also attempted to provide suitable political institutions for both the English- and French-speaking populations.

This new political system lasted less than 50 years. By the 1830s, the populations of the two Canadas had matured and could no longer be kept in the straight jacket designed for them in 1791. Resistance to the authority and elitism of the British and indigenous oligarchs led to rebellions in both Canadas. Each was quickly suppressed, leaving distrust and fear of the English for many years among the French in Lower Canada.

The British soon sent the Earl of Durham to assess the situation and prescribe remedies for the management of the obstreperous colonies. His report, completed in 1839, is one of the most important documents in Canadian history. He was sympathetic to the complaints of both the French- and English-speaking populace, but implicit in the report was the suggestion that the French population in Lower Canada be assimilated by the English. One important recommendation, soon effectuated, was the reunification of Upper and Lower Canada to form again a "Canadian" colony.

The period of the 1830s was a social watershed for the French Canadian population of Lower Canada. The high birth rate soon exceeded the carrying capacity of the St. Lawrence Lowland and resulted in a massive outmigration of people. What began as a trickle in the 1830s, became a flow in the 1840s and a flood in the 1850s; this emigration lasted for decades thereafter.

Many unskilled rural folk were lured to the towns and cities, especially Quebec City and Montreal, thus reducing significantly the proportion of the English population in urban areas. Aided by church leaders who hoped to avoid the trend toward urbanization, which they perceived as corrupting and degrading, huge tracts of marginal land north of the St. Lawrence Valley and in the Lake St. John region were opened up for settlement. The population spilled into the Ottawa Valley, eastern Ontario, and south of Montreal. Attracted especially by jobs in the textile factories, countless thousands moved southward to the border areas and to towns in the northern United States. In New England they added an entirely new ethnic element to many staid towns and villages. Others sought their fortunes on the western frontier in both Canada and the United States. By the 1860s, the French Canadian population, while still heavily concentrated in

the St. Lawrence Lowland, had become much more geographically dispersed.

The new political system in the "Canadian" colony during this time had become virtually unworkable. Thanks in part to the events in the United States, a solution was found or — as some would stress — forced upon the colonies. Faced with increased British indifference or exasperation with their colonies in North America and the considerable threat from the still expansionist-minded United States, the leaders during the early 1860s sought a political system that would provide a stronger united front against the U.S. After several years of negotiations, it was agreed that a quasi-federal system should be formed, in many aspects independent of Great Britain. French Canadian leaders in particular agreed to the plan on the condition that the Canadian colony once again be divided to create a political entity for the French Canadian population in the St. Lawrence Valley and environs. With the passage of the British North America Act on July 1, 1867, by a somewhat relieved British Parliament, the new provinces of Ontario and Quebec, a rather hesitant Nova Scotia and New Brunswick joined to form the Dominion of Canada.

One of the first actions of the new Canadian government was to purchase Rupert's Land, in what is now northern Canada, from the Hudson's Bay Company and eventually give portions of it to Ontario and Quebec. The provinces of Quebec and Ontario were enlarged many times as a result.

From the time of the first settlements, there has never been a contiguous French Canada. This fact was even more evident during the latter half of the 19th century. French Canada by 1870 had expanded considerably from its colonial cores along the St. Lawrence and Annapolis Valleys. While the new Province of Quebec remained indisputably the heartland, other distinctive and distinguishable French Canadian areas had developed primarily as the result of migrations from Quebec to adjacent regions of Ontario and to northern and southwestern sections of that province. A new Acadian heartland had developed and expanded in northern New Brunswick. Acadian areas were also located in southern Nova Scotia and eastern Prince Edward Island. The Canadian West had isolated pockets of French Canadians as well. In fact, colonies had been established in the early 1800s on Hudson's Bay Company land on the prairie fringe, primarily to exploit the fur trade.

The itinerant Métis were a significant ethnic element of the fur trading population. Because they were French speaking and Roman Catholic, these fiercely independent descendants of the coureurs de bois identified with the French rather than the English peoples of Eastern Canada. For more than a century, they had been principals in the western fur trade, living in many cases an Indian way of life.[4] As fur trading declined during the first half of the century, the Métis became progressively more dependent upon the buffalo for their livelihood. By the 1860s, however, the number of buffalo had declined significantly due to over exploitation and the impact of waves of settlers pouring into the Great Plains and prairies.

The policy — some would say obsession — of the new central government in Ottawa was to occupy the Canadian West as quickly as possible to keep the region from being colonized by U.S. settlers, who had already begun to move northward across the border. Unfortunately, these settlers — European, U.S. and Canadian alike — came in direct contact and conflict with the Métis. At first diplomatically, and later violently, the Métis resisted attempts by

the aggressive central government to destroy the buffalo and their habitat in order to build railways, subdivide the land and impose a sedentary way of life upon them.

In 1868, the government attempted to establish a new province out of the Red River settlement headquartered at Fort Gary (later Winnipeg), where the Métis were heavily concentrated. Under Louis Riel, their undisputed leader and one of the few free spirits and eccentrics in Canadian history, the Métis formed their own provisional government and insisted upon entering the Canadian union on their own terms. Several ugly incidents occurred before an agreement was negotiated that recognized Métis land claims and guaranteed French language rights and the free practice of the Roman Catholic Religion. This led to the passage of the Manitoba Act and the creation of Canada's fifth province.

Riel reappeared in Saskatchewan during the mid-1880s to defend and protect once again the Métis and Indian way of life in what was then the "western frontier." Riel was captured, convicted of treason and hanged. This action elicited a considerable backlash against the English, particularly in Quebec, since Riel's hanging was seen as an act of irrational vengeance against French Catholic people by the English Protestant establishment of Ontario.

Riel's demise marked the end of Indian, Métis and French power in the West and paved the way for the abrogation of their civil rights in Manitoba a few years later. The francophones were subsequently overwhelmed by the massive infusion of English colonists; by 1900, only isolated pockets were left, mainly in southern Manitoba near Winnipeg (St. Boniface).

By the turn of the century, the Province of Quebec was increasingly identified as *the* heartland of French Canada. The French population continued to reproduce at an enormous rate, equivalent to the indigenous growth of the English population

[4]In 1860, there were in all of the "Canadian" West only 2,000 English-speaking settlers and Hudson's Bay Company employees, many thousands of Indians, and approximately 6,000 Métis.

plus immigration. While this distinctive province functioned comfortably within the Canadian Confederation, its societal development and politics periodically diverged from the central government.

Outmigration from the farms in Quebec to the cities, the West or the United States continued. The church-inspired frontier development policy north of the St. Lawrence had failed to attract enough settlers to have any significant impact upon this rural-to-urban rush. Foundries, breweries, textile factories and banks, controlled primarily by the English minority in the province, flourished in the towns and cities. Although a small industrial and financial French Canadian bourgeoisie existed in the urban areas, the majority of the population was still rural and tied closely to the church and *la terre*. Quebec, therefore, entered the 20th century different in many respects from the English-speaking provinces. It lagged behind the rest of Canada, especially Ontario, in industrial development with a people still clinging to traditional values and life-style.

WHO AND WHAT ARE CANADIANS OF FRENCH ANCESTRY?

U.S. residents have often been intrigued, if ·not puzzled and confused, by the terminology used to describe the people living in Canada or regions therein. We will focus on the evolution of terms describing the ethnic identity of Canadian people of French origin, especially those in the Province of Quebec.

The word *Canadian* in an ethnic, geographical, linguistic and political sense has had an interesting and somewhat inconsistent history as it relates to Canada's two founding nations. The term gradually emerged during the early 1700s to refer to native born people of French or French-Indian ancestry, most of whom were hunters or peasants living a subsistent exis-

tence on the seigneuries owned by the aristocrats. Therefore, until the conquest, there existed two terms in Nouvelle France, *les français* and *les Canadiens*.[5]

After 1763 no common terminology evolved to describe both founding peoples of Canada. *Canadien* was associated primarily with French-speaking people, who constituted a majority of the population of British North America from 1763 to about 1850. According to les Canadiens, all other inhabitants of the British colonies— United Empire Loyalists, British settlers and indigenous English alike—were *les Anglais*. The English-speaking population commonly referred to themselves during the early years as English, British North Americans, or more often, British and not Canadian, although they were residing in a "Canadian" colony. According to them, the French-speaking population of the St. Lawrence Lowland and the Maritimes were *The French*. Thus, the descriptive terms used by both linguistic groups to describe each other were ethnic, rather than political, linguistic or geographical.

This tendency was reinforced during the "British period" by the fact that the names of the colonial entities located in the northeastern half of the continent were constantly changing. For example, the territory along the St. Lawrence was, over the span of 100 years, referred to sequentially as the Quebec Colony (1767–1791), Lower Canada (1791–1841), the Canada Colony — Canada East (1841–1867) and the Province of Quebec (1867 to the present). Obviously, insufficient time elapsed for any territorial or politically based terminology to develop and be perpetuated.

Confederation, the establishment of distinct provincial subunits and the emergence after 1850 of an English-speaking

---

[5]The term *habitant*, from the French word *habitué* or permanent resident, has also been used for centuries in reference to the francophone peasant of rural Quebec. It is now considered pejorative since the majority of the Quebec population has for many decades lived in cities.

majority in Canada as a whole, resulted in and indeed necessitated, the development of new terms to describe the two founding nations. To distinguish themselves from *les autres*, Canadians of French origin became known as *les Canadiens français* (French Canadians). Little attempt was yet made to identify with any specific region of French Canada. The remainder of the population, the economic and demographic majority of British extraction, referred to themselves as *Canadians* or, less frequently, *English Canadians*. Thus, for the first time, there were linguistic undertones to the ethnic terms. The singular term *Canadian*, used in a political and territorial sense, was still less important.

The 20th century has seen many changes in what Canadians call themselves and are referred to by others, particularly in French Canada. A trend has emerged to identify the two founding groups by language, territoriality and ethnicity.[6] During the past two decades the terms francophone and anglophone have been used and accepted more and more, not only because of a desire by political and cultural leaders to separate language from nationality, but also to accommodate the many "new Canadians" who have arrived in Quebec during this century.[7]

Traditionally, a *Québécois* was from the City of Quebec (in the same way a *Montréalais* is a Montrealer and a *Beauçeron*, someone from the Beauce, south of Quebec City). Gradually, Québécois has evolved to

be used in a wider geographical, broader political and, in some cases, specific ethnic context, although the last is far more subtle. Some Quebec nationalists argue that Québécois are Quebec residents of French origin, distinct from English-speaking Quebecers and immigrants, as well as from francophones residing outside Quebec. This interpretation became common during the first decade of the Quiet Revolution (1960–1970), when the francophone population was demonstrating a greater self-confidence. The tendency was to identify as Québécois rather than French Canadian—as a majority within the territory of Quebec rather than as a perpetual minority in Canada.

Another interpretation — used principally to avoid accusations of ethnocentrism and to allay fears of sensitive immigrants and anglophones who claimed they were being relegated to second class citizenship—is that anyone residing in Quebec is a Québécois, i.e., Québécois has a territorial but not necessarily an ethnic or linguistic meaning.

To many non-francophones, however, this new Québécois identity is grounded in ethnic factors that go beyond French language capability and residency in Quebec. Non-francophones — even native-born anglophones whose roots in Quebec go back several generations — have difficulty in accepting designation as Québécois people. Irrespective of social class and ethnic backgrounds, they have found it easier to identify as Canadians rather than Québécois. Many francophone Quebecers, on the other hand, consider themselves Québécois first and Canadians second.

Concurrent with the acceptance of Québécois to characterize all or a part of the Quebec population is the development of other terms to identify francophones living outside the Province of Quebec. In areas or provinces where recognizable and cohesive French-speaking communities

---

[6]Derogatory terms abound among the French- and English-speaking communities. Commonly used by the English have been *frog, pea soup,* and *Pepsi,* in reference to the French Canadians—in the first case because *soupe aux pois* had for generations comprised an important part of the *Canadian* diet, and in the last example because Quebec residents allegedly drank a lot of Pepsi (an observation made decades before the "Pepsi challenge") English Canadians were *Têtes Carrées* (square heads), *Coup de Thé* (tea drinkers), *les Anglais*, or sometimes *les maudit Anglais* (the damn English).

[7]Immigrants whose language of daily use is neither English nor French are referred to in Quebec as *allophones*.

still exist, provincially focused terms such as *Franco-Manitobans* and *Franco-Ontarians* are now widely accepted.

The term *Acadian* has survived for centuries. While the vast majority of people who call themselves *Acadians* are francophones and identify with the Province of New Brunswick where most now reside, other small Acadian communities are located throughout the Maritimes. Thus, Acadian is primarily an ethnic term, with no implicit political, geographical or linguistic connotation.

In sum, the term *Canadien* in the traditional sense is now an anachronism in Quebec (except for hockey teams) and will likely disappear when the older generation passes away. Also, French Canadian is being used less frequently in Canada as people seek to be identified within a specific ethnic or provincial context.

QUEBEC—THE HEARTLAND OF FRENCH CANADA

Quebec is the *sine qua non* of French Canada and the continued existence of distinctive francophone communities elsewhere in Canada is closely linked to the political importance of Quebec within the Canadian federal system. Francophones, who are a minority of the population of Canada, constitute a large majority of Quebec's inhabitants. Therefore, the mere survival, let alone the growth and development, of French-speaking communities outside of Quebec has benefited recently from pressures emanating from Quebec to legitimize the French language and the unique culture of the predominantly French-speaking residents within the province. Official bilingualism cannot be achieved in Ontario without constant demands from Quebec that the distinctiveness of the French Québécois be acknowledged in the constitutional framework of Canada. French Canadians residing outside Quebec, therefore, are both hostages to and beneficiaries of a strong Quebec that continues to remain part of Canada. Quebec, historically the source of population replenishment throughout French Canada, the place where priests and teachers to staff French Canadian schools and hospitals were often recruited, today is the primary source of French language TV and radio programming for Radio-Canada. Indeed, without Quebec, a "French Fact" could no longer exist in North America.

The Quiet Revolution in Quebec And Its Aftermath

In a narrow political sense, the so-called Quiet Revolution in Quebec began with the provincial electoral defeat of the Union Nationale (UN) government in 1960 at the hands of the Quebec Liberal Party led by Jean Lesage. This change was revolutionary indeed and unleashed a chain of social, economic and political events that rocked the very foundations of Quebec society and indeed of Canada itself.

During its heyday from the mid-1930s through the 1950s, the Union Nationale propagated to its electorate the conservative French Canadian nationalist themes of ruralism, clericalism, anti-communism and provincial autonomy. These were seen as keys to the survival of a distinctive French Canadian community in the face of predominantly anglophone and non-Catholic North American patterns of urbanization, industrialization and consumerism, values it should be noted compatible with those of the church at that time. Maurice Duplessis, the long-time leader of the UN and premier for nearly 20 years (1936–39, 1944–58), facilitated church control over an autonomous network of educational, health and social welfare institutions, and even trade unions, as well as cooperative savings and loan associations. The Quebec state invested comparatively little public money in social and economic development. Quebec was then a place of English bosses, union-busting, low wages and limited overall economic opportunity for its French-speaking majority. Also characteristic of this period was censorship of films and books, repression of women (who could not vote in Quebec provincial elections until 1944), high birth and infant mortality rates, and suppression of religious minorities and political dissent. Equally important was the classical Catholic humanist educational structure, which was out of step with the economic requirements of an increasingly urban society and industrial economy. The Duplessis era had to end before the Quiet Revolution could begin.

The 20th century revolutions in communications and transportation, which physically brought the people of North America closer together much more frequently than ever before, helped open the door to the Quiet Revolution. Tourists and investors came to Quebec from other parts of Canada and from the United States; French Québécois moved from the country to live in cities in ever-larger numbers and traveled to the U.S. more often. The people were now more frequently exposed to the materialist aspirations, life-styles, urban values, practices, institutions and standards of the anglophones from elsewhere in North America. There was also growing interaction with foreign science and technology. People with new skills, philosophies and concepts eroded traditional support for an insular French Canadian community. This contributed to an undercurrent of rising expectations among French Québécois that living standards should be improved. Such feelings were manifested more graphically by labor unrest and bitter strikes in Quebec, as future leaders of French power, such as Pierre Trudeau, expressed their impatience with the machinations of the Duplessis government, the irrationalities of the old order and the irrelevancy of traditional French Canadian nationalism.

The sudden death of Duplessis in September 1958, in effect, marked the end of an era in Quebec. Duplessis's power had been absolute and no future leader had been groomed. Within two years an election was held and the UN was out of power. Led by Jean Lesage, the Parti Libérale du Québec (PLQ) now guided the destinies of this provincial state as it entered the fateful era of the Quiet Revolution.

According to Lesage and his colleagues, the machinery of the Quebec state had to be modernized through vigorous state intervention to catch up with other regions of Canada and the United States. The expansion of Hydro-Quebec through nationalization of anglophone-owned and managed private hydroelectric power companies outside of Montreal epitomized the new aggressive economic order in the francophone community.

The PLQ won the 1962 provincial election on the issue of nationalization. Opposition UN critics saw it as an act hostile to the principles of free enterprise; anglophone business critics doubted the ability of a predominantly French-speaking state monopoly to manage its affairs competently. In fact, Hydro-Quebec proved to be a manifestation of state capitalism, rather than the vanguard of socialism in Quebec, and a symbol of the neo-nationalism, which has focused on dynamic growth rather than on stagnant survival.

The new technocracy in Quebec quickly concluded that to avoid either folklore status or breakdown of a sense of community in the province, the economic, social and political institutions would have to be modernized; and an impartial, professional and nonpartisan civil service put into place. This was set in motion in the first phase (1960–1962) of the Quiet Revolution, and the process of modernization, institutional reform and *rattrapage* (catching up) was continued during the second Lesage Liberal government in Quebec City (1962–1966).

In large measure, the growth of the public bureaucracy was due to an increased awareness of structural barriers to equitable francophone participation and decision making in the private sector of the economy proportionate to their numerical majority status in Quebec itself. Francophone involvement in the corporate boardrooms of Canada as a whole was even more inadequate. The Royal Commission on Bilingualism and Biculturalism, created by the Pearson government in Ottawa, documented the nature and measured the extent of economic and other forms of discrimination against French Canadians during the early to mid-1960s. Recommendations focused on how to alleviate the tensions that were bound to occur due to gross disparities of income and opportunity between the two founding peoples of Canada. Such official disclosures contributed substantially not only to the rise of "French power" in Ottawa, but also to the emergence of explicitly separatist political parties in Quebec. The election of Pierre Trudeau as leader of the Liberal Party of Canada and soon as prime minister (1968) came about in part because to many French Québécois he represented the native son in Ottawa who would direct tangible advantages to them. At the same time, to Anglo-Canadians concerned about what they construed as a rising separatist threat to Canadian national unity from Quebec, Trudeau, an avowed federalist, represented someone who would resist pressures from Quebec for special consideration and privileges.

By the mid-1960s, widespread dissatisfaction with the established order had developed in Quebec. One indicator was the emergence of minor separatist political parties on the provincial political scene. Another was the number of constitutional options short of political sovereignty widely debated among the Quebec intelligentsia as well as among journalists and technocrats. These included demands for special status for Quebec within Canada, official recognition of two nations within the Canadian state, and an associated states confederal arrangement between Quebec and the other provinces.

A variety of governmental and extra-governmental expressions of discontent with the federal constitution, established during the 1960s, paralleled dynamic social change in the province. The Quebec Civil Code, unique in Canada, was updated, and the rights of women were strengthened. During this period Quebec joined the Canada-wide hospital insurance and medicare programs. Though the UN was elected to office (1966–70), in part due to fears by more conservative francophone voters in rural areas and small towns regarding the nature and pace of change, the new government continued to implement basic reforms; namely, a non-partisan civil service, more crown corporations and continued state involvement in economic and social development. The reforms of the Quiet Revolution were irreversible; the "Old Quebec" of the Duplessis era would not return.

Nationalism in Quebec

Nationalism has been a factor in Quebec politics since the establishment of an elected legislative body in Lower Canada in 1791. However, it has constantly needed redefinition to enable temporarily ascendant social classes within the French-speaking community ideologically to justify responses to changing economic, social and political circumstances. These dominant elements within francophone Quebec society have monopolized the symbols of nationalism to advance the interests of a certain class, but always in the name of the society as a whole. This task was made easier by the threats to the positions of all social classes within the Franco-Quebec community posed by the powerful presence of anglophones in Quebec as well as in the rest of Canada.

The traditional survival-oriented French Canadian nationalism heavily stressed the virtues of interethnic élite accommodation. The French Canadian petty bourgeoisie embraced the illusion that conservative nationalism would somehow be able to protect them from the economic depredations of cultural rivals, while at the same time legitimizing their middle class status within the francophone social structure.

During the 1960s, the new urban and suburban middle classes became the ascendant strata in French Quebec society. Its intellectuals, journalists and public bureaucrats articulated a new version of Québécois nationalism which varied substantially from that of the past. While they still sought to convey a sense of continuity to such segments of society as small scale urban entrepreneurs and small-town notables, who needed reassurance in the face of a destabilizing industrial socio-economic order, they also sought to legitimize the aspirations of the upwardly mobile middle class, the primary francophone beneficiaries of these relatively abrupt socio-economic transformations. These Quebec intellectuals were linked with or had disproportionate access to the mass media, the labor activists and the rapidly growing junior colleges and universities. Thus, their nationalist idealism paved the way for the emergence of a multiclass francophone clientele, which merged to form the Parti Québécois in the late 1960s under the leadership of the charismatic former

Liberal, René Lévesque. Politicians in Ottawa and the Montreal anglophone business establishment finally began to take heed, perhaps a little too slowly.

The PQ took advantage of widespread disaffection with Canadian federalism in Quebec throughout the 1960s and into the 1970s. Sometimes this dissatisfaction was expressed in a variety of extralegal ways by such socialist- or nationalist-oriented groups like the *Societé Saint Jean Baptiste*, the *Mouvement National des Québécois*, the *Mouvement pour l'Integration Scolaire* (French unilingualism in education), and the trade unions. Such elements in French Quebec society were impatient with both the rate and the direction of social and economic change. Thus, even in the face of the October Crisis of 1970, which involved the kidnapping of a British Trade Commissioner plus the abduction and murder of the Quebec Minister of Labor by a small cell of Nationalist radicals, the PQ was able to present itself as a credible and authentic but nonviolent Québécois nationalist alternative. It played a vital role in helping to maintain the legitimacy of the Quebec political system during the 1970s, when the restless energies of a growing number of radicalized francophones, frustrated by a process of change that did not correspond to the expectations unleashed by the Quiet Revolution, sometimes went beyond constitutional means to obtain redress of grievances.

The Contemporary Quebec Economy

The Quebec economy continues to exhibit an overdependence on the traditional, obsolete, labor-intensive manufacture of textiles, clothing, footwear, leather goods and furniture, which has contributed to consistently higher unemployment and lower overall productivity than exists in Ontario. Moreover, such manufactured goods have been marketable throughout

Canada only because of protectionist tariffs, quotas and other trade barriers. In
addition, the Quebec economy has been
dependent upon exports of unprocessed or
semiprocessed products, such as iron ore,
asbestos, pulp and paper, copper, zinc and
gold — primarily to the U.S. — and massive sales of hydroelectric energy to New
England and New York. A substantial alu-
minum industry has developed due to the
availability of relatively cheap hydroelectric energy and the proximity of U.S.
markets. Many of these economic activities have involved capital investments
by English Canadian and foreign firms
(primarily U.S.-based multinational corporations) and recent joint ventures involving private foreign and Canadian firms
as well as Quebec crown corporations.

Quebec needs more modern, inter-
nationally competitive, export-oriented
industries that utilize her comparative advantages (e.g., an abundance of relatively
cheap renewable hydroelectric energy and
access to large markets). Most of the markets for Quebec-produced electronic
goods, office and communications equip-
ment, ground transport locomotives, pro-
cessed natural resources, etc., are and will
be in the U.S., not in the rest of Canada.
Already, one-half of Canada's aerospace
industry is concentrated in Quebec. Moreover, for high tech industries to evolve in
the large scale required, major United
States participation will continue to be
needed in the forms of expanded private,
direct investment, joint ventures, North
America-wide marketing systems and
technical expertise.

The Role of the English in Quebec

The non-French population in Quebec is
no longer homogenous. Since World War
II, it has been increasingly difficult to
characterize the English-speaking community in anything other than vague

terms, because ethnic and religious diversity has been more characteristic of the
anglophone minority than of the francophones. This situation exists because
the English community, primarily due to
its domination of the provincial economy,
has had a much greater capacity to attract
immigrants. Now there are fewer Quebec
residents of British descent than there are
of other non-French ethnic origins (see
table I).

Two important factors have facilitated
the development of a network of presti-
gious educational and other social institutions controlled by the anglophone (i.e.,
the ethnic English) community: the cultural environment in North America and
the better-than-average economic opportunities available to native-born English-
speaking inhabitants. Every anglophone
can acquire a university education in English in Quebec. Anglophones have their
own radio and television stations, li-
braries, newspapers, bookstores, etc. They
have used their own financial resources to
establish health and social welfare institutions and services of high quality.

Compared with the francophone majority, anglophone Quebecers have been
heavily involved in industrial, commercial and banking enterprises, and in
ownership of capital. The economic sectors under British anglophone influence
are characterized by a higher level of productivity and are more monopolistic, oligopolistic and capital-intensive, while the
manufacturing spheres dominated by
Jews, Greeks and other ethnic groups have
tended to be smaller, less efficient, more
labor-intensive, more competitive and less
oligopolistic. Furthermore, large anglo-
phone-controlled enterprises are generally
more involved in exports to the U.S. than
the small- and medium-sized ethnic or
francophone family firms in Quebec.

Quebec nonfrancophones constitute a
pyramid of groups vertically ordered in

Table 1. Population of Quebec: Ethnic Origin, 1851–1981

Census Year	French %	British %	Other %	Total
1851	669,887 (75.2)	215,034 (24.2)	5,340 (0.6)	890,261
1871	929,817 (78.0)	243,041 (20.7)	18,658 (2.3)	1,172,858
1901	1,322,115 (80.2)	290,169 (17.6)	36,614 (2.2)	1,648,938
1931	2,270,059 (79.0)	432,726 (15)	171,470 (6.0)	2,874,255
1951	3,327,128 (82.0)	491,818 (12.1)	236,735 (5.9)	4,055,681
1971	4,759,360 (79.0)	640,045 (10.6)	628,360 (10.4)	6,027,765
1981	5,105,670 (80.2)	487,385 (7.7)	776,015 (12.1)	6,369,070

Source: Government of Canada, *Census of Canada*, 1851–1981.

relation to status and power, ranging from an Anglo-Protestant charter group at the summit, to Third World groups like Haitians and Vietnamese at the bottom. The Anglo-Protestant charter group, the first nonfrancophone cultural entity to settle in Quebec, has actively participated in the economic development of the province. It has managed to retain control over outside cultural groups seeking integration or assimilation into the English-speaking community. Partly in response to the rise of contemporary French Québécois nationalism and partly due to their disproportionately high representation in the professional, managerial and self-employed occupational strata, the Anglo-Protestant charter group increasingly has had to share control of many anglophone institutions with such upward mobile nonfrancophone groups as the Jews and Irish Catholics. Non-British-, non-French-ancestry persons have also been amenable to political mobilization by the "Establishment" against both Law 101 (which, among other measures, made French the only official language in the province) and the PQ separatist option, and for the PLQ.

Members of the anglophone community in Quebec, especially the ethnic English, have been leaving the province in increasing numbers since the beginning of the Quiet Revolution. A combination of factors has contributed to this exodus — the general movement of the economic center of Canada westward to Toronto and even to Calgary, Edmonton and Vancouver; the general malaise of the Quebec economy; the heavy personal income tax in Quebec compared with other areas of Anglo-North America; and the manifestations of French Quebec nationalism — which have significantly reduced the power of the English community. For generations, anglophones have left Quebec in significant numbers for other parts of North America, but official language legislation during the 1970s has substantially reduced the pattern of replacement through the anglicization of allophones and the immigration of anglophones. As a result, anglophones have declined vis-à-vis francophones, especially during the last 15 years.

The number and proportion of the total population of non-French, non-English

"OF COURSE IT'S DIFFICULT FOR OUTSIDERS TO GRASP THE SUBTLE COMPLEXITIES OF THE SITUATION HERE IN QUEBEC"

Aislin/Montreal Gazette

ethnics in Quebec have also changed significantly during the past decade. Recent immigrants, such as the Portuguese and Greeks, are for the most part still allophones, have not yet integrated into either of the two principal linguistic groups, and with the francophones have increased in number. On the other hand, the "old guard" ethnic communities, such as the Jews, Germans, Poles and Ukrainians, have declined. Most of these people had integrated into the anglophone community by 1960. Since they are "marketable" throughout North America and share the anxieties of the ethnic English, they have joined the general anglophone exodus in substantial numbers. This trend does not bode well for the anglophone community in Quebec in the long run, especially in areas outside the region of Montreal where

numbers have declined precipitously of late.

FRENCH CANADA — THE FUTURE

In Ottawa, the era of French power at the pinnacle of the political order is drawing to a close. A greater preoccupation with the health of the overall Canadian economy, rather than constitutional issues where Quebec played a central role, is likely. It is true that the present Progressive Conservative Prime Minister Brian Mulroney, whose party won an impressive 58 out of 75 seats in Quebec in the general election of September 1984, is fluently bilingual, comes from Quebec, and strongly supports the Trudeau vision of one Canadian nation and two official languages from sea to sea. Nevertheless, the predominantly English Canadian coalition of forces, which the 211 Tories elected to the 282 seat House of Commons represent, will compel this PC government to be more responsive to other regions, economic interests and priorities. True, there will be no major roll-backs in the implementation of the federal official languages policy. However, a state of affairs where French Quebecers occupied such crucial cabinet portfolios as prime minister, finance, energy and justice *at the same time* will not return very soon. Other factors related to the decline of French power in Ottawa are the decrease in the francophone percentages of the total Canadian population; the continuing anglicization of substantial proportions of French-origin Canadians in areas geographically contiguous to Quebec and elsewhere; and the rise in the numerical and hence political, economic and cultural significance of non-British, non-French ancestry groups in English Canada.

For all these reasons, the avenues of political accommodation between federal and English Canadian provincial governments to meet the concerns and needs of French Canadian minorities outside of Quebec will be less open. Rather, Franco-Ontarians and Manitobans, seeking from their provincial governments official status for the French language, minority language education rights and social services in their own language, will be more prone to resort to the courts, which now have the power of judicial review, instead of political processes. With the sense of urgency concerning the Quebec question now removed, and with French Quebec's political potency in decline, federal governments will be less inclined to pressure provincial governments on French Canadian minority language questions. Moreover, regardless of the political orientation of future Quebec governments, the long-term trend since the 1920s on the part of Quebec to abandon its role as guard-

ian of French Canada as a whole will likely continue.

The Parti Québécois, nearing the end of its second mandate, is at an extremely low ebb in popularity due to such factors as conflicts with labor, scandals, the unpopularity of the independence movement, discouragement among party militants and economic stagnation. Therefore, does the seemingly inevitable demise of the PQ as a governing political force signify the decline of nationalism? We think not. People were predicting oblivion for nationalism in Quebec at the outset of the Quiet Revolution on the premise that prosperity, modernization and social mobilization were anathema to nationalism per se rather than merely to its conservative and reactionary French Canadian "survivance" forms.

One imponderable in the equation is the future political allegiance of the francophone entrepreneurial and professional classes in the private sector who are growing in numbers, as well as in social prestige and political influence. They are now a welcome and integral part of what had previously been an anglophone-dominated private sector. Will they execute a *new* Quiet Revolution in the 1990s by serving as the vanguard of an antistatist and antiseparatist as well as antinationalist trend, which will give the final coup de grace to the *projet national* aspirations of the 1960s? Or will their growing sense of political and economic efficacy pave the way to political rupture with the rest of Canada?

What one sees at present is continuing adherence, by these private sector francophone entrepreneurial and professional classes and their young aspiring recruits, to the thesis of a strong Quebec in a revised federal Canada. It remains to be seen whether English Canada will come forth with sufficient constitutional concessions to satisfy the present strongly antiseparatist but still predominantly Québécois nationalist orientations of these crucial segments of French Quebec society.

To complicate matters further, a Liberal government in Quebec, if elected in late 1985 or early 1986, would probably be unable to resolve what are fundamentally structural rather than merely cyclical economic problems. The renewed federalist option policy of Robert Bourassa, the resurrected leader of the PLQ, mandates continued dependence upon the initiatives of the Canadian economy as a whole. More fundamentally, no major Canadian federal or Quebec provincial government has seriously acted upon a strategy to reverse substantially the growing interdependence between the Canadian/Quebec and U.S. economies. Thus, in one sense, neither the renewed federalist option nor the political sovereignty of Quebec vis-à-vis Canada are relevant, since Quebec's collective economic well-being will in numerous respects ultimately be tied to decisions made in the U.S. or in Canada as a whole. The Bourassa Liberals acknowledge this North American fact of life by advocating increased exportation of hydroelectric energy southward and an improved climate for large-scale direct investment by primarily U.S. multinational corporations. Even the PQ acquiesces when its Minister of International Trade advocates, as he has done recently, a common North American economic accord with the United States. Whatever political party holds power in Quebec City between now and the year 2000, the "U.S. Card" will be played more and more frequently.

Pro-U.S. orientations on the part of all major competing segments of the Quebec political elite will continue. These will be shared by an increasingly U.S.-influenced francophone rank and file. Because they speak a different language and because the perceived source of their political as well as economic subordination is English Can-

ada, francophone Québécois élites tend to downplay any purported U.S. threat to their distinctive way of life. From the perspective of Franco-Québécois, whether their preferences are separatist or federalist-nationalist, the U.S. offers the potential of serving as an effective economic counterweight to English Canada. Ultimately this could mean more political leverage for Quebec vis-à-vis Ottawa. At the same time, close economic and, if possible, political ties with France are seen by political élites of most persuasions as desirable because they provide a potential countervailing cultural counterweight to the economic, scientific and technological preponderance of the United States.

There will continue to be growing acceptance throughout English Canada of the predominantly French character of Quebec. Future court decisions and Quebec Liberal modifications regarding presently controversial education and public advertising provisions of Law 101 will further reinforce tacit acquiescence by all Canadians of Canada's duality, of which Quebec is a unique component. Nevertheless, a myriad of Canada-Quebec as well as intra-Quebec French-English issues will continue to provide ample nourishment to francophone Québécois nationalist movements of varying ideological emphases and degrees of commitment to political sovereignty. Rank-and-file English Canadians, especially in Quebec itself, will take much longer to reconcile themselves to the new French Quebec, and will unintendedly fuel periodic re-emergence of French Québécois nationalist political discourse.

French Quebec will survive and develop more readily than French Canada — that is clear. However, it is too early to tell whether this French Québécois culture will be able to successfully incorporate the highly diverse ethnic, racial and religious character of its recent immigrants, let alone its anglophone minority. In a sense, the vertically segmented social structure that existed in Quebec prior to the 1960s, where anglophones bore the "burden" of pluralism in their schools, hospitals, etc., must now be projected to characterize the francophone society of the future primarily because of Law 101. The policy of francization of Third World immigrants not only will add substantial numbers to the francophone proportion of the population, but will also result in far greater interaction with the host francophone Québécois society. In addition, the people will compete, in French, for jobs that are increasingly hard to find in a relatively weak economy. These non-French Canadian ethnic francophones represent values, attitudes and beliefs that differ from those of their hosts. Certainly French Quebec political elites and opinion leaders have appeared to make every effort to create the institutional supports for and a climate of opinion favorable to their successful assimilation. Nevertheless, these elites do not necessarily speak for the francophone rank and file who, for example, continue to support maintenance of a denominational, government-subsidized school system, rather than a non-denominational one. Such a preference works at cross purposes with the franco-assimilationist goals of the progressive Quebec elite and opinion leaders.

French language and culture will continue to flourish in Quebec as the centerpiece of a dynamic community that refuses to die à la solution Louisianienne (Louisiana solution for the Cajuns and Creoles) or that refuses to accept mere folkloric status. Outside of Quebec, the multiculturalism policy of the Canadian government to some extent helps to mask the reality of Anglo-conformity in the rest of Canada. The most that can be achieved, outside the areas adjacent to Quebec in Ontario and New Brunswick, will be peripheral, marginal status. Even French Canadians themselves will be able to attach only a low value to the French language in the scientific, technological and economic domains and a high value to the English language. Such hard facts are irreversible, despite the panoply of publicly subsidized as well as private cultural and social institutions in French Canada devoted to perpetuation of the myth of equality between the two founding peoples throughout the country. CBC television stations beaming Montreal-produced Radio-Canada French language programs to Toronto and Vancouver, and even the rapidly growing popularity in English Canada of French-immersion primary and secondary school programs cannot stem the inexorable tide of assimilation in most areas outside of Quebec.

Bibliography

Arnopoulos, Sheila M., and Dominique Clift. *The English Fact in Quebec.* Montreal: McGill-Queens University Press, 1980.

Bernard, A. *What Does Quebec Want?* Toronto: James Lorimer, 1978.

Bouchard, René, ed. *Culture Populaire et Littératures au Québec.* Saratoga, CA: Anma Libri, 1980.

Cardinal, Claudette. *The History of Quebec: A Bibliography of Works in English.* Montreal: Concordia University, 1981.

Carrier, R. *La Guerre Yes Sir!* Translated by Sheila Fischman. Toronto: Anansi, 1970.

Desbarats, P. *René: A Canadian in Search of a Country.* Toronto: McClelland & Stewart, 1977.

Hero, Al O., Jr., and Marcel Daneau, eds. *Problems and Opportunities in U.S./Quebec Relations.* Boulder, CO: Westview Press, 1984.

Lévesque, René. *My Quebec.* Translated by Gaylord Fitzpatrick. Toronto: Methuen, 1979.

MacLennan, Hugh. *Two Solitudes.* Toronto: Macmillan of Canada, 1945.

Milner, H. *Politics in the New Quebec.* Toronto: McClelland & Stewart, 1978.

Sénécal, André, and Nancy Crane. *Quebec Studies: A Selected Annotated Bibliography.* Burlington: University of Vermont, 1982.

Trofimenkoff, Susan M. *The Dream of Nation: A Social and Intellectual History of Quebec.* Toronto: Macmillan of Canada, 1982.

Trudeau, P. E. *Federalism and the French Canadians.* Toronto: Macmillan of Canada, 1972.

Wade, Mason. *The French Canadians, 1760–1967* (2 vols.). New York: St. Martin's Press, 1968.

Student Activities

Beach and Lubin provide a comprehensive look at French Canada from the time of its inception to the present day. They examine it from a historical perspective including a look at the impact of the Roman Catholic Church, and a contemporary examination of the role of politics and the economic state of affairs.

The authors share their insights about the current status of French Canadians, probe the issues surrounding nationalism and analyze the role of the English in Quebec. They conclude with predictions about French Canada's future.

As students pursue the following activities, they should imagine French Canada as a mosaic, consisting of a wide variety of ever changing social, political, historical, and economic factors that have contributed to the emergence of French Canada as we know it today.

1. What Is Different?

Secure the English and French versions of the Canadian National Anthem. How are they alike? How are they different? Construct a chart like the one below depicting the likenesses and differences. Be ready to discuss how the anthem reflects Canada's history and its people.

ENGLISH AND FRENCH VERSIONS OF CANADIAN NATIONAL ANTHEM	
Likenesses	Differences

2. Could (Should) the Province of Quebec Survive As an Independent Entity?

Consider this question carefully. Several members of your class can volunteer to serve as panel members or the panel can be appointed by your teacher.

Unlike debaters, panel members are not under pressure to take extreme viewpoints or to disagree with what other members have expressed. The purpose of a panel is to facilitate consensus, develop a compromise, or recognize differences that can't be immediately resolved.

If you are a panel member, you need to think clearly about your views and prepare adequately so that your presentation will be objective. While each panelist can specialize in gathering information on a particular aspect of the topic, the presentations should be interrelated so that an exchange of ideas is easily facilitated. One student should be selected as chairperson and another as recorder. Each panelist should have a specified number of minutes for making his or her presentation; time should also be allotted for interaction and questions.

You should decide the role of the audience (members of the class who are not panelists). For example, should they be encouraged to ask questions during the panel discussion? Should they be responsible for note taking? In any case, they too should be knowledgeable about the topic.

3. How Has the Church Affected French Canada's Development?

The church hierarchy defined the Roman Catholic faith as the protector of the French language in Canada. What are the facts? What are your opinions? Investigate the role of the church in French Canada's development. Seek information through books and people. Invite religious leaders in your area to your classroom to share their insights regarding this issue. Some sample questions are: Do you see the church as having had that much power? Why? Why not? Does the same situation exist today? Why? Why not? How has Catholicism (or any religion) impacted on your community? If the church's position has become strengthened or weakened over time, what have been the contributing factors?

4. What Do You See as the Ten Most Significant Events in the Development of French Canada?

Using a variety of library sources, identify the 15 to 20 key events that have played a major role in molding French Canada into what it is today. Then, using your best judgment, narrow the list down to ten. Place these ten events on a time line. Be able to defend each chronologically and in terms of its significance in French Canada's development. Next, working in pairs, share your time lines. Try to convince your peer that the events you selected are the most significant. The challenge is to see if you can arrive at consensus! If you can, work with your classmate in constructing a new time line. Be prepared, regardless of the outcome, to present the results to the class. If time permits, see if the class can reach consensus on what are the most significant events and why.

5. Check Out the Economic Situation in Quebec.

According to Beach and Lubin, the Quebec economy continues to exhibit an overdependence on traditional, obsolete, labor-intensive manufacture of textiles, clothing, footwear, leather goods and furniture. What does this mean? The following words are associated with economics:

Domestic demand
Foreign demand
Consumer spending
  Service expenditures
  Spending for durable goods
  Spending for nondurable goods
Unemployment
Construction expenditures
  Business
  Residential
Imports
Exports
Inflationary trends

See if you can locate data about Quebec for each of the above words or categories. (If you want an extra challenge, try to add other categories.) Use a variety of library sources and resource people to assist you with this assignment.

On the basis of the data gathered, how does Quebec benefit or lose by being one province out of ten in Canada? Defend your position.

6. What Does Art Tell You About a Place?

Probably the most powerful influences on Canadian painting have been the land and the people. The land's being so different from Europe has always fascinated painters. The uniqueness of the Indians, frontiersmen, trappers and Quebec habitants have provided fresh material for the artist. The early painters tended to see the new land and its people through European eyes and, because they were trained in Europe, these artists often imposed European techniques on Canadian subject matter.

Study the painting "Habitant Farm" by Cornelius Krieghoff carefully. List your observations. List the questions that are raised in your mind. Examine the painting for European influences and list them. Then do some research to learn more about the artist. Be ready to share your insights with your fellow students.

For those of you who are especially interested in art, select one of the following artists and find out about his or her works and the artist's life. Write a one-page position statement explaining why you would (or would not) want to spend a day with this person if he or she were alive.

Some Famous Canadian Artists of the
19th and 20th Centuries

Artists to learn more about:
Robert Bateman (1930-   )
Emily Carr (1871-1945)
Maurice Cullen (1866-1934)
Lawren S. Harris (1885-1970)
A. Y. Jackson (1882-1974)
Paul Kane (1810-1898)
Cornelius Krieghoff (1815–1872)
William Kurelek (1927-1977)
J. E. H. MacDonald (1873-1932)
Norval Morrisseau (1932-   )
Tom Thomson (1877-1917)

7. What Does It Mean?

How would you interpret the following statement: "French Canadians residing outside Quebec are both hostages to and

Courtesy of National Gallery of Canada

Habitant Farm by Cornelius Krieghoff, 1854

beneficaries of a strong Quebec that continues to remain part of Canada."

On a piece of paper, write down your interpretation. Then survey ten people. Determine how their responses are similar or dissimilar. Be prepared to share the data with your classmates. Gather information to support its true meaning.

If you have the opportunity, interview a French Canadian in your community. Elicit his or her reaction to the statement.

8. Would You Like to Interview a Historical Character?

This technique can make history more interesting by creating a living process in your classroom.

Choose a historical person who figures prominently in French Canadian history. Then select one person in the room (or a history buff in the community) to assume the identity of the historical figure. That person (after having sufficient time to learn about the character) will be interviewed by the class.

If you are an interviewer, review the basic techniques of conducting an interview. The class should then agree on several general questions to be asked. To make the experience more meaningful, assume the roles of reporters.

During the interview, raise your hands and be recognized just as reporters do in an actual news conference. The individual playing the role of the historical character should attempt to imitate the types of responses the actual character would give.

When the interview is concluded, write a newspaper article covering the event and share it with a peer.

Resources for Studying About Canada

The Canadian Studies projects and Canadian consulates listed below are a valuable resource for Canadian studies. Both are capable of providing social studies educators with a wide variety of free and inexpensive materials for classroom use and for curriculum development activities. It should be noted, however, that the Canadian Studies projects listed here are representative of such activities throughout the United States; some offer a wide variety of outreach activities for schools. Canadian consulates are excellent sources of free films, bulletins and pamphlets on Canada.

CANADIAN STUDIES PROJECTS IN THE UNITED STATES

Dr. Pat Curada
Canadian Studies Program
Boise State University
Boise, ID 83725
(206) 385-1011

Dr. John Myers, Director
Bridgewater State College
Bridgewater, MA 02324
(617) 697-8321

Dr. Earl Fry, Coordinator
Canadian Studies Programme
Department of Government
Brigham Young University
Provo, UT 84602
(801) 378-3377

Professor Peter Kresl
Department of Economics
Bucknell University
Lewisburg, PA 17837
(717) 524-1476

Professor Thomas G. Barnes/
Professor Victor Jones
Co-Chairmen
Canadian Studies Program
Institute of International Studies
University of California, Berkeley
215 Moses Hall
Berkeley, CA 94720
(415) 642-6749

Professor Wayne C. Muller
Canadian Studies Program
Department of Government
California State University
6000 J Street
Sacramento, CA 95819
(916) 454-6504

Dr. Michael G. Fry, Director
School of International Relations
University of Southern California
University Park – MC 90089
Los Angeles, CA 90089
(213) 743-6278

Professor Henry King
U.S. Director
Canadian/US Law Institute
Case Western Reserve Law School
Cleveland, OH 44106
(216) 368-3294

Dr. John Ruggie, Director
Canadian Studies Programme
Columbia University
New York, NY 10027
(212) 280-4616

Professor Ross C. Horning, Jr.
Department of History
Creighton University
2500 California Street
Omaha, NE 68178
(402) 449-2651

Dr. Richard Leach, Director
Canadian Studies Programme
2101 Campus Drive
Duke University
Durham, NC 27706
(919) 684-2765

Dr. Henry Kennedy, Director
Canadian Studies
University of Central Florida
Orlando, FL 32816
(305) 275-2079

Dr. Harold Gortner
Canadian Studies Programme
George Mason University
440 University Drive
Fairfax, VA 22030
(703) 323-2001

Professor Seyom Brown
Centre of International Affairs
Harvard University
1737 Cambridge, MA 02138
(617) 495-2125

Dr. Charles Doran
Academic Director
Center for Canadian Studies
Johns Hopkins University (SAIS)
1740 Massachusetts Ave., N.W.
Washington, DC 20036
(202) 785-6292

Professor Victor Konrad
Director
Canadian-American Centre
University of Maine at Orono
Orono, ME 04473
(207) 581-2222

Professor George T. Sulzner
Director
Five College Consortium
University of Massachusetts
Thompson Hall
Amherst, MA 01003
(413) 545-0410

Professor Victor Howard, Chairman
Committee for Canadian-American Studies
Michigan State University
East Lansing, MI 48823
(517) 353-9349

Professor Robert M. Stern
Head, IPPS International Program
The University of Michigan
1516 Rackham Building
Ann Arbor, MI 48109
(313) 764-3490

Dean Bernard O'Kelly
Canadian Studies Committee
University of North Dakota
Box 8038, University Station
Grand Forks, ND 58202
(701) 777-2749

Professor Hans J. Peterson
Department of Social Science
Southern Montana College
Havre, MT 59501
(406) 265-7821

Dr. Barry Farrell, Director
Canadian Studies Programme
236 Scott Hall
Northwestern University
Evanston, IL 60201
(312) 869-4326

Dr. George Maloof
Canadian Studies Programme
Plymouth State College
Plymouth, NH 03264
(603) 536-1550

Dr. Robert W. Thacker
Canadian Studies Programme
St. Lawrence University
Canton, NY 13617
(315) 379-6296

Dr. Richard Tobin
Dept. of Political Science
Canadian Studies Programme
SUNY Buffalo
Buffalo, NY 14214
(716) 636-2133

Dr. Richard Beach, Director
Centre for the Study of Canada
SUNY Plattsburgh
Plattsburgh, NY 12901
(518) 564-2086

Dr. Oren Davis, Director
Canadian Studies Programme
Trinity College
Burlington, VT 05401
(802) 658-0337

Dr. E. J. Miles, Director
Canadian Studies Programme
University of Vermont
Burlington, VT 05401
(802) 656-3062

Professor Robert Monahan,
Chairman
Committee on Canadian & American Studies
Western Washington University
Bellingham, WA 98225
(206) 676-3284

Professor H. B. Westerfield
Dept. of Political Science
Canadian Studies Programme
Yale University
New Haven, CT 06502
(203) 436-8737

CANADIAN CONSULATES IN UNITED STATES

Canadian Embassy
1746 Massachusetts Ave., N.W.
Washington, DC 20036
Phone: (202) 785-1400

Canadian Consulate General
400 South Omni International
Box 56169
Atlanta, GA 30303
Phone: (404) 577-6810

Canadian Consulate General
500 Boylston St.
Boston, MA 02116
Phone: (617) 262-3760

Canadian Consulate General
One Marine Midland Center, Suite 3550
Buffalo, NY 14203
Phone: (716) 852-1247

Canadian Consulate General
310 South Michigan Ave., Suite 1200
Chicago, IL 60604
Phone: (312) 427-1031

Canadian Consulate General
Illuminating Bldg.
55 Public Square
Cleveland, OH 44113
Phone: (216) 771-0150

Canadian Consulate General
750 North St. Paul, Suite 1708
Dallas, TX 75201
Phone: (214) 922-9806

Canadian Consulate General
1920 First Federal Bldg.
1001 Woodward Ave.
Detroit, MI 48226
Phone: (313) 965-2811

Canadian Consulate General
510 West Sixth St.
Los Angeles, CA 90014
Phone: (213) 627-9511

Canadian Consulate General
15 South Fifth St.
Minneapolis, MN 55402
Phone: (612) 333-4641

Canadian Consulate General
Ste 2110
International Trade Mart
2 Canal St.
New Orleans, LA 70130-1459
Phone: (504) 525-2136

Canadian Consulate General
1251 Ave. of the Americas
New York, NY 10020
Phone: (212) 586-2400

Canadian Consulate General
3 Parkway Bldg.
Suite 1620
Philadelphia, PA 19102
Phone: (215) 561-1750

Canadian Consulate General
One Maritime Plaza, Ste. 1100
Golden Gateway Center
San Francisco, CA 94111-3468
Phone: (415) 981-2670

Canadian Consulate General
412 Plaza 600
Sixth & Stewart
Seattle, WA 98101
Phone: (206) 223-1777

PROVINCIAL GOVERNMENT "HOUSES" IN THE U.S.

Delegations du Quebec

Ms. Jean Morin, Délégué
Délégation du Québec
Peachtree Ctr. Tr., Suite 1501
230 Peachtree St. N.W.
Atlanta, GA 30303

M. Pierre Baillargeon, Délégué
Délégation du Québec
Exchange Place, 19th floor
Boston, MA 02109

Ms. Jean Berard, Délégué
Délégation du Québec
35 East Wacker Dr., Suite 2052
Chicago, IL 60601

Mr. Roland Berland, Délégué
Délégation du Québec
World Trade Ctr., Space 100
2050 Stemmons Fr., Box 581038
Dallas, TX 75258

Mr. Jean Goyer, Délégué
Délégation du Québec
303 Quest, Rue Vermilion
Lafayette, LA 70501

Mr. Pierre Jolin, Délégué
Délégation du Québec
Broadway Pl., Bureau 1520
700 South Flower Street
Los Angeles, CA 90017

Ms. Rita Dionne-Marsolais,
Déléguée Générale
Délégation Générale du Québec
Rockefeller Ctr., 17 W. 50th St.
New York, NY 10020

Mr. Pierre Valiquette,
Conseiller
Bureau du Tourisme du Québec
1300, 19th St. NW Suite 220
Washington, DC 20036

Ontario

800 Third Avenue
Suite 2800
New York, NY 10022
Phone: (212) 308-1616

1 Embarcadero Center
Suite 2107
San Francisco, CA 94111
Phone: (415) 989-0850

Prudential Building
Suite 4066
800 Boylston Street
Boston, MA 02199
Phone: (617) 266-7172

Alberta

3535-333 South Grand Avenue
Los Angeles, CA 90071
Phone: (213) 625-1256

5444 W. Heimer Road
Suite 1425
Houston, TX 77056
Phone: (713) 871-1604

General Motors Building, 23d Floor
767 5th Avenue
New York, NY 10153
Phone: (212) 759-2222

INDEX ————————————————

A
Acadia, Acadians, 42, 44–45, 90–92, 94, 97.
Acid Rain, 3, 7, 16, 51, 56–69.
Alberta, 10, 27, 31, 38, 41, 43, 45, 48, 50, 51, 77.
  See also Prairie provinces.
Annapolis Valley, 90, 93.
Architecture, 11, 14–15.

B
Bathurst, New Brunswick, 12.
Bilingualism, 3, 6–7, 12–13, 17, 30, 52–53, 79,
  89–106.
Bourassa, Robert, 105.
Borden, Robert, 24, 26.
Brebeuf, Jean de, 21.
British Columbia, 23, 31, 41–47, 49–50, 74–77,
  79, 84.
British heritage, 6, 11, 12–14, 21, 80.
British North America Act (1867), 5, 23, 32, 82,
  93.
British royal family, 13–14, 28, 32.

C
Cabot, John, 20, 89.
Calgary, 10, 47–49, 102.
Canada Act (1791), 21, 92.
Canadian Shield, 32, 37–38, 39, 44, 45, 49–51.
Cape Breton Island, 20, 89, 91.
Cape Tormentine, 12.
Cartier, Georges Etienne, 23.
Cartier, Jacques, 20, 80, 89–90.
Catholic religion, 15–16, 20–21, 23, 44, 81, 91,
  92, 94, 98, 102.
Chaleur Bay, 12.
Champlain, Samuel de, 20, 79–80, 90.
Churchill, 50.
Computers, computer simulation, 7, 56–69.
Cordillera, 37, 39–45, 49.

D
Dawson City, 24, 79.
Diefenbaker, John, 27.
Distant Early Warning (DEW) line, 4.
Duplessis, Maurice, 28, 97–99.
Durham, Lord (Earl of), 22, 93.

E
Economy, Canadian, 1–4, 8, 16, 23, 26, 28–32,
  39, 47, 49–50, 51, 98–99, 104.
Edmonton, 47–48, 52, 102.
Ellsmere Island, 38.

Erie, Lake, 22, 45. See also Great Lakes.
Eskimo, 7, 53, 75, 77–78.
Ethnic groups, 6, 11, 24, 27, 32, 49, 83–89, 96,
  101–102.
  Chinese, 4, 7, 11, 83.
  Germans, 45, 83, 103.
  Greeks, 101, 103.
  Haitians, 102.
  Italians, 27.
  Japanese, 7, 84.
  Jews, 101, 103.
  Koreans, 7, 84.
  Poles, 27, 103.
  Portuguese, 103.
  Russians, 24, 27, 83.
  Ukrainians, 45, 83, 103.
  Vietnamese, 102.

F
FLQ, See Front de Liberation du Quebec.
Fraser, Simon, 22, 79.
Fredericton, New Brunswick, 39.
French Canada, 6, 7–8, 80, 89–106.
French heritage, 6, 12–13, 16, 20–21, 80.
Frobisher, James, 22.
Front de Liberation du Quebec (FLQ), 28, 82.
Fundy, Bay of, 12, 44.

G
Gaspé Peninsula, 12, 44, 89.
Ghent, Treaty of, 22.
Government, Canadian, 3–4, 16, 22–23, 28,
  32–34, 93–106.
Graphics, computer, 67.
Great Lakes, 12, 21, 37–38, 40–41, 45, 50, 51,
  80, 91, 92.
Great Slave Lake, 50–51.

H
Halifax, 38, 47–48.
Hamilton, 47.
Hudson Bay, 37, 39, 49–50, 80, 91.
Hudson's Bay Company, 22, 45, 80, 93–94.
Hydro-Quebec, 98.

I
Immigration, migration, 6–7, 21–22, 24, 27, 33,
  44–47, 80, 83–84, 91, 94–95, 101–103,
  105–106.
Indians, 20–21, 23, 74–78, 80–81, 89–91, 94.
Inuit, 46, 75, 77–78.

National Council for the Social Studies
Publications Staff for *Canada in the Classroom*
Charles R. Rivera, *Editor and Director of Publications*
Anne Janney, *Associate Editor*
Mildred Edwards, *Indexer, Proofreader*
Cover Design by Mene Santana